Amigurumi

HOLIDAY HATS

for 18-Inch Dolls

20 Easy Crochet Patterns for Christmas, Halloween,
Easter, Valentine's Day, St. Patrick's Day & More

Linda Wright

In memory of Grandma R. and her pretty hats

Also by Linda Wright
Toilet Paper Origami
Amigurumi Toilet Paper Covers
Amigurumi Golf Club Covers
Amigurumi Christmas Ornaments
Amigurumi Animal Hats for 18-Inch Dolls
Honey Pie Amigurumi Dress Up Doll with Picnic Play Set
Honey Bunny Amigurumi Dress Up Doll with Garden Play Mat
Chef Charlotte Amigurumi Dress Up Doll with Tea Party Play Set

All rights reserved. No part of this book may be reproduced, stored in a retrieval system, or transmitted, in any form or by any means, electronic, mechanical, photocopying, recording, or otherwise, without prior written permission from the publisher. Permission is granted to photocopy patterns and templates for the personal use of the retail purchaser.

Lindaloo Enterprises is not affiliated with American Girl®.

Copyright © 2015 Linda Wright
Edition 1.1

Lindaloo Enterprises
P.O. Box 90135
Santa Barbara, California 93190
United States
sales@lindaloo.com

ISBN: 978-0-9800923-9-4
Library of Congress Control Number: 2015907349

Contents

Introduction 5   General Directions 6

Valentine 21

Hearts Around 24

Shamrock 27

Top Hat 29

Funky Bunny 32

Easter Bonnet 35

Pumpkin 44

Easter Chick 38

Stars & Stripes 41

Witch 47

Black Cat 49

Devil 52

Turkey 55

Santa 58

Reindeer 60

Poinsettia 63

Christmas Tree 66

Party Hat 75

Ginger Bread Girl 69

Buckle 'n Belt 72

Resources 78 Templates 79 Featured Yarn 82

Introduction

Imagine your doll dressed as a reindeer, topped with a turkey, looking like a leprechaun, or pretty as a poinsettia! Festive hats for the holidays make dressing dolls so much fun! Hats complete an outfit like icing on a cake. They have the power to turn even the simplest doll clothes into a stylish fashion statement or a costume. In this collection of hats, you will find styles ranging from whimsical to beautiful—and always colorful.

Amigurumi (ah·mee·goo·roo·mee) is a Japanese term for cute crocheted objects, animals or people. It is done by crocheting in a continuous spiral using one primary stitch—the single crochet—which makes it easy to master. *Amigurumi Holiday Hats for 18-Inch Dolls* is perfectly suited for the beginning crocheter. These patterns use the most elementary stitches and techniques while delivering an adorable result in a short amount of time.

These hats were designed for my American Girl® dolls, but there are many other 18" dolls with a similar 12" head circumference. Measure your doll just above the ears. If slight adjustments are needed, going up or down a hook size or adjusting your tension (tightness) will make a hat larger or smaller.

The patterns in this book appear in calendar order starting with Valentine's Day in February through Christmas in December plus everything in between. You will find hats for Halloween, Easter, St. Patrick's Day, Independence Day and Thanksgiving—plus a Party Hat for New Year's Eve or birthdays.

I have used easy-to-find worsted weight yarn in this book, but holidays are all about sparkle and shine, so this would be an ideal time to try any novelty metallic yarns that catch your eye at the yarn shop. Be sure to choose category #4 worsted. Shimmery purchased baubles provide additional ways to enhance your hats and bring on the bling. For example, try decorating the Christmas Tree hat with sequins, beads or buttons rather than French Knots.

For more delightful doll hats, check out my companion book, *Amigurumi Animal Hats for 18-Inch Dolls*!

General Directions

If you're new to crocheting, or if you need to brush up, the following pages include instructional diagrams for the stitches used in this book.

If you like to learn by watching, YouTube.com is a treasure trove of excellent crocheting tutorials. To find what you need, just search on the stitch you want to learn and, for the best results, include "crochet" in your search. For example, magic ring crochet (also known as the magic circle or magic loop), single crochet, or loop stitch crochet. Several embroidery stitches are used for finishing touches on the hats and these can also be found demonstrated on YouTube, for example, the French knot.

For a hand-picked source of tutorials, I have assembled a collection of my favorites on Pinterest. You can view them at www.pinterest.com/LindalooEnt/ on boards named "Amigurumi Tutorials" and "Embroidery Tutorials". There you can watch demonstrations for the stitches and techniques needed to make amigurumi holiday hats for your dolls.

Amigurumi is meant to be crocheted rather tightly. Be sure to check your gauge at the beginning of each pattern.

This book uses U.S. crochet terms. If an instruction says sc, that is a U.S. single crochet—or a U.K. double crochet. Please refer to the stitch diagrams on the following pages to be sure you are making the stitches as intended.

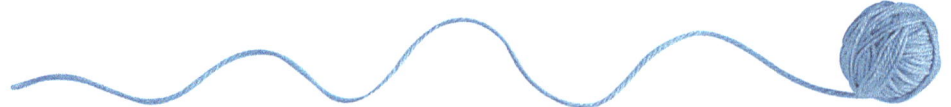

Supplies

Yarn

All of the yarn used to make these hats is soft worsted-weight yarn marked as number 4. Look on the label for the yarn weight symbol containing a "4" in the middle of a ball of yarn. Soft yarns frequently include "soft" in their name. I primarily use Caron "Simply Soft", Red Heart "Soft", Lion Brand "Vanna's Choice" and Lion Brand "Cotton-Ease". A yarn that is made of acrylic fibers, or acrylic blended with cotton or wool, is an ideal choice because the hat will be colorfast, washable and hold its shape well. The yarns that I used for these projects are listed in the Resources section at the back of the book.

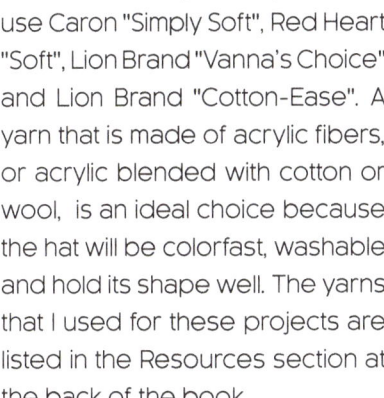

Scissors

You will need a small pair of sharp scissors.

Crochet Hook

All of these patterns have been designed for a U.S. H/8 (5 mm) crochet hook. You may need to go up or down a hook size to obtain the gauge. My absolute favorite hook is the Clover Soft Touch Crochet Hook (pictured below, center). I love the ergonomic grip which keeps my hand from going numb when crocheting for long periods of time and the shape of the head which inserts easily into a stitch.

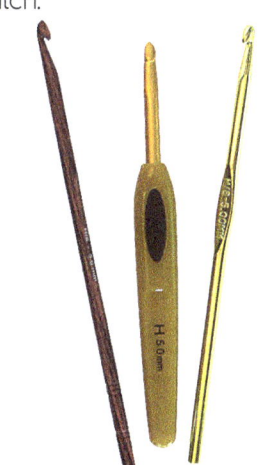

Yarn Needle

Yarn needles, or jumbo tapestry needles, have a large eye and a blunt point. They are made from metal or plastic. You will use one to sew the various pieces of your hat together and also to finish it off by weaving the loose ends into your work.

Stitch Markers

Stitch markers are used to keep track of where a round or row of crochet begins and ends. You can use a safety pin, bobby pin, paper clip or purchased stitch markers. I recommend the locking stitch markers that are shaped like safety pins. They are very easy, secure and convenient to use. Making the correct number of stitches is important, so count to double check if ever you're not sure.

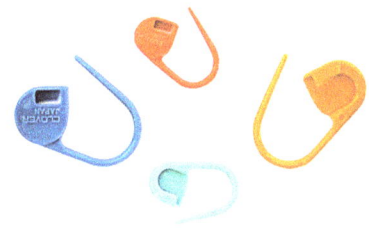

Buttons

Buttons are used for most of the eyes. Sometimes a single set of buttons is used and sometimes buttons are stacked for a 2-tone effect. When buttons are stacked, use flat buttons with 2 or 4 holes in the surface. When unstacked, shank buttons can be used.

General Directions

Disappearing Ink Marking Pen

This terrific marking tool is a felt-tipped pen with ink (usually purple) that disappears in a day or so. Purchase it at a fabric store, craft store or online.

Row Counter

Well worth the investment, a row counter keeps track of what round of the pattern you are crocheting. A pencil and paper can also be used.

Straight Pins

Use standard dressmaker's pins or long corsage pins to hold pieces in place before sewing.

Sewing Needle & Thread

You will need these sewing box basics.

Styrofoam Ball

A 4-inch styrofoam ball makes a convenient hat form. Place hats on the ball to pin auxiliary features in place and mark their position.

Removable Notes

Use small sticky notes to keep track of your place in a pattern. Every time you complete a round or a row, move the note down to reveal the next line of instructions. I wouldn't work without one!

Stuffing

There are a few stuffed pieces in these patterns. Polyester fiberfill is my favorite stuffing material. This can be purchased by the bag at craft stores. One bag will go a long way! Scraps of yarn can also be used.

Ruler

For measuring and marking.

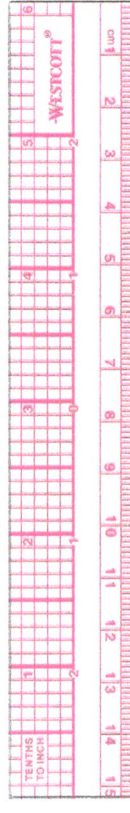

Crochet Stitches

SLIP KNOT

This is used to make a starting loop on the crochet hook.

1. Make a loop about 5 inches from end of yarn. Insert hook in loop and hook onto supply yarn (yarn coming from ball) at A.

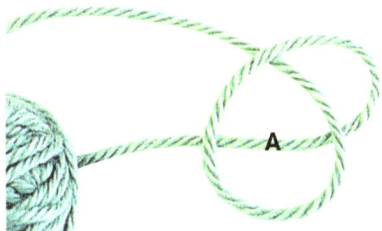

2. Pull yarn through loop.

3. Pull yarn ends to tighten loop around hook.

CHAIN (CH)

Start with a slip knot on hook.

1. Bring yarn **over** hook from back to front. Catch yarn with hook and pull it through the loop —

to look like this. One ch is done.

SINGLE CROCHET (SC)

This simple stitch is the primary stitch for amigurumi.

1. Insert hook in designated stitch. Note: Put hook under **both loops** that form v-shape at top of stitch unless otherwise instructed.

2. Yarn over and pull through the stitch (A).

You now have 2 loops on the hook:

3. Yarn over and pull through both loops on hook.

4. You now have 1 loop on hook and the sc stitch is done.

General Directions

HALF DOUBLE CROCHET (HDC)

1. Yarn over and insert hook in designated stitch.

2. Yarn over and pull through the stitch (A).

You now have 3 loops on hook:

3. Yarn over and pull through all 3 loops on hook (A, B & C).

4. You now have 1 loop on hook and the hdc stitch is done.

DOUBLE CROCHET (DC)

1. Yarn over and insert hook in designated stitch.

2. Yarn over and pull through the stitch (A).

You now have 3 loops on hook:

3. Yarn over and pull through 1st 2 loops on hook (A and B).

You now have 2 loops on hook:

4. Yarn over and pull through both loops on hook.

5. You now have 1 loop on hook and the dc stitch is done.

TRIPLE CROCHET (TR)

Also known as Treble Crochet.

1. Yarn over **twice** (from back to front) and insert hook in designated stitch.

2. Yarn over and pull through the stitch to have 4 loops on hook:

General Directions   11

2. Yarn over and pull through 1st 2 loops on hook (A and B).

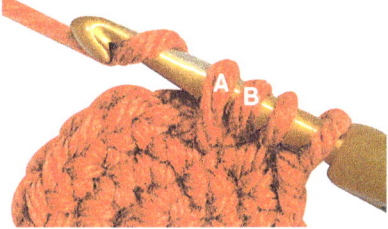

You now have 3 loops on hook:

4. Yarn over again and pull through next 2 loops on hook (A and B) **twice** —

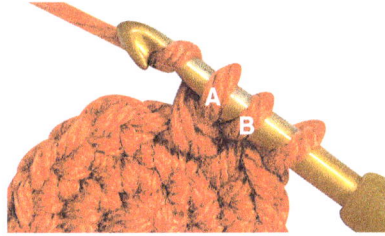

5. You now have 1 loop on hook and the tr stitch is done.

SINGLE CROCHET DECREASE (SC2TOG)

The instruction "sc2tog" means to use single crochet to join 2 stitches together. It is a way to decrease or make the item smaller.

1. Insert hook in stitch, yarn over and pull up a loop — to look like this:

2. Insert hook in next stitch, yarn over and pull up a loop — to look like this:

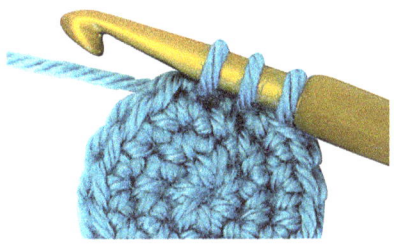

3. Yarn over and pull through all 3 loops on hook — to look like this. The sc2tog is done.

SLIP STITCH (SL ST)

1. Insert hook in stitch. Yarn over and pull through stitch and through loop on hook (A and B).

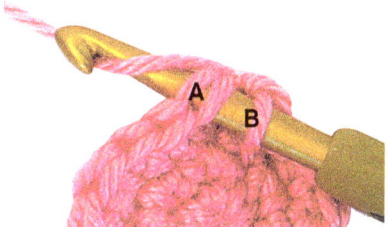

2. The sl st is done.

Techniques

★ MAGIC RING

Most all of my amigurumi begins with the magic ring. This is the way to get a nice, neat center when crocheting in the round. The magic ring is an adjustable loop that you can tighten — like magic! It's not difficult — and well worth it. (An alternative to the magic ring, if desired, is to chain 2. Then begin Round 1 by working into the 2nd chain from the hook instead of the ring.)

1. Make a ring a few inches from end of yarn. Grasp ring between thumb and index finger where the join makes an X. Insert hook in ring, hook onto supply yarn at Y and pull up a loop —

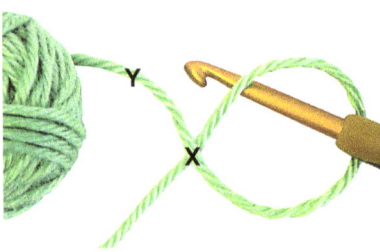

to look like this.

2. Chain 1 —

to look like this. This chain does not count as a stitch.

3. Insert hook into ring so you're crocheting over ring and yarn tail. Pull up a loop to begin your first single crochet —

and complete the single crochet.

4. Continue to crochet over ring and yarn tail for the specified number of single crochets for the 1st round.

5. Pull tail to close up ring. To begin the 2nd round, insert hook in 1st stitch of 1st round (see arrow).

BEGIN 2ND RND HERE

WORKING IN THE ROUND

Working in the round means crocheting in a continuous spiral. Most amigurumi is worked in this manner.

General Directions

USING STITCH MARKERS

It can be tricky to keep track of your place when working in the round, so be sure to use a stitch marker. The pattern will remind you! Place the stitch marker in the first stitch of a round — after completing the stitch. When you've crocheted all the way around, remove the stitch marker, make the next stitch, and replace the marker in the stitch just made. This will be the first stitch of the next round.

WORKING IN LOOPS

When a single crochet stitch is made, you will see 2 loops in a v-shape at the top of the stitch. To crochet the patterns in this book, insert your hook under **both loops** unless instructed otherwise. Crocheting in the "front loops only" or the "back loops only" is sometimes used for a different effect.

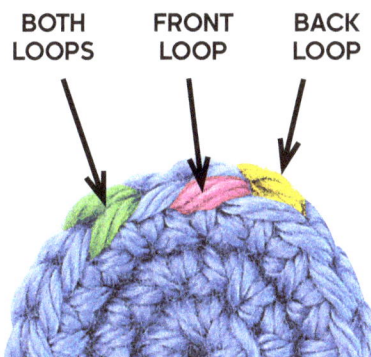

BOTH LOOPS FRONT LOOP BACK LOOP

MARKING THE EAR FLAPS

Counting clockwise from long tail of Hat, put stitch markers in stitches 10, 18, 37 and 45. Crochet Ear Flaps into the 7 stitches between each set of markers, not including the marked stitches. (See purple stitches in photo below.)

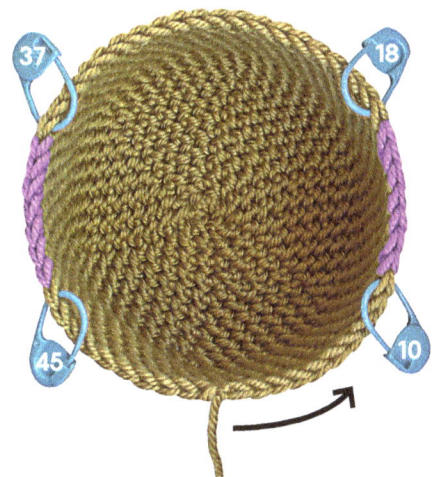

ATTACHING WITH SC

Attach yarn to hook with Slip Knot. Insert hook in indicated stitch. Complete sc as shown in Single Crochet tutorial, page 9,

CHANGING COLORS

To change color while single crocheting, work last stitch of old color to last yarn over, yarn over with new color and pull through both loops on hook to complete the stitch.

FASTENING OFF

This is the way to finish a piece so that it won't unravel. When you're done crocheting, cut the yarn and leave a tail. Wrap the tail over your hook and pull it all the way through the last loop left on your hook. Pull the tail tight and it will make a knot.

SMOOTHING THE EDGE

When fastening off, the knot can make a small bump in the edge of your work so that, for example, a round shape will not look as round as it should. To make the edge smooth, thread the long tail in a yarn needle and insert the needle down through the center "V" of the next stitch. This little step makes a big difference.

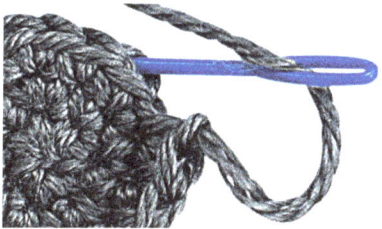

General Directions

TWISTED CORD TIE

1. With crochet hook, pull 6 yarn strands through tip of Ear Flap —

and pull 1 side of loop all the way through until lower ends are even.

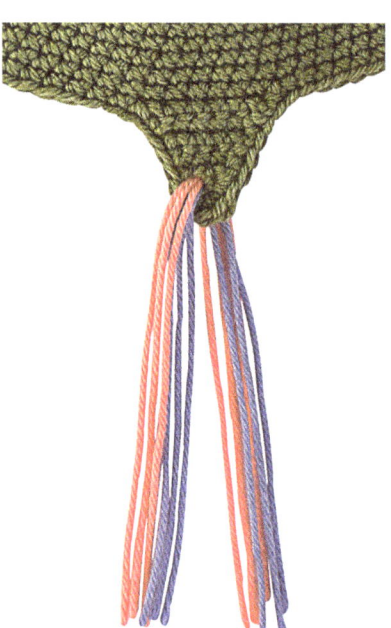

2. Place hat on a firm surface and weigh it down with a heavy book. Divide yarn into 2 groups of 6 strands. If 2 colors are used, make each group the same color.

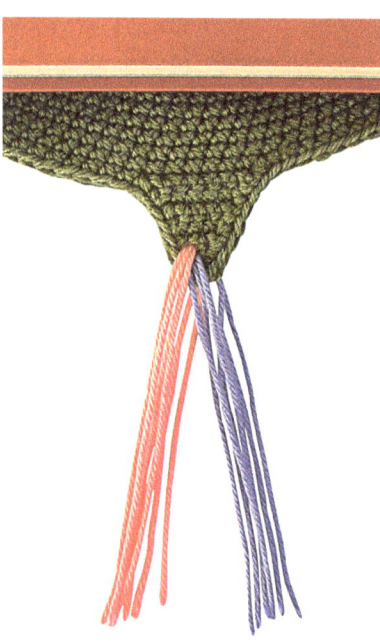

3. Hold a group in each hand grasping about 2 inches from Ear Flap — and twist yarn to the right.

4. When yarn has a good tight twist, wrap right group over left group —

and wrap **right over left** a few more times until all twisted yarn is wrapped.

5. Move your hands down 2 more inches, twist yarn and repeat Step 4. Continue twisting and wrapping until near end of strands. Tie all strands together with an overhand knot 6 inches from tip of Ear Flap. Trim ends even.

General Directions

SMALL POM POM

To embellish the ends of Twisted Cord Ties.

1. Copy and cut out 2 Small Pom Pom templates (see page 79). Glue templates to lightweight cardboard. (A cereal box is a good weight.) Cut along black lines. Hold cardboard templates together so that notches align. Wrap yarn evenly around ring, sliding yarn through notch and slit to begin each wrap.

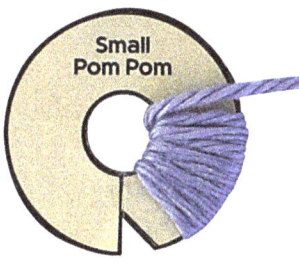

Wrap until inner circle is **almost filled** with yarn.

2. Insert Twisted Cord Tie into center of cardboard ring. Put 1 leg of scissors between cardboard rings and cut yarn apart around outer edge.

3. Slide a scrap of yarn between cardboard rings and tie the ends together very tightly.

4. Remove cardboard. Slide Pom Pom down cord to cover knot of Tie. Fluff yarn into a ball and trim surface into a nice, round shape.

LARGE POM POM

To embellish the top of a Hat.

1. Copy and cut out 2 templates for Large Pom Pom (see page 79). Glue templates to lightweight cardboard. (A cereal box is a good weight.) Cut along black lines. Hold cardboard templates together so that notches align.

2. Wrap yarn evenly around ring, sliding yarn through notch and slit to begin each wrap. Wrap until inner circle is **filled** with yarn.

3. Put 1 leg of a pair of scissors between cardboard rings and cut yarn apart around outer edge.

4. Slide a scrap of yarn between cardboard rings and tie the ends together very tightly. Leave long ends to use for tying Pom Pom to Hat.

5. Remove cardboard. Fluff yarn into a ball and trim surface into a nice, round shape.

General Directions

FRINGE

1. Follow pattern instructions for length and quantity of yarn strands to be used. Put hook through desired stitch, catch strand(s) in the middle and pull part way through stitch to make a loop. (Photos below show fringe being made with 2 yarn strands.)

2. With hook in loop, lay yarn ends over hook.

3. Pull yarn ends all the way through loop. Take hold of ends and pull tight.

COUNTING ROUNDS

Periodically, it is good to count your rounds to ensure your place in a pattern. Fortunately, rounds are clearly defined and counting is easy. Each round makes a ridge. A groove separates the rounds. You need only to count the ridges. Take a look at the photo below to see that the circle has 5 rounds.

ASSEMBLING

The assembly stage of amigurumi hatmaking is an exciting time. This is when all pieces are sewn together and the project blossoms in cuteness! Thread a yarn needle with the long tail of your auxiliary piece (nose, heart, flower, etc.) and use a whip stitch or running stitch to sew it to the hat. It's good to temporarily pin your pieces in place beforehand to decide where you like them the best.

WEAVING IN ENDS

The final assembly instruction for every pattern is to weave in the ends. This is the way to hide and secure all of your straggly yarn tails. Thread the yarn end into a yarn needle, then skim through the back of the stitches on the wrong side of your work. Continue for about 2 inches, then turn and double back to lock the yarn into place. Trim the end close. When you turn your work to the right side, you should not see the woven ends. They should be tucked into the middle of your crocheted fabric.

CLEANING

If you have used washable yarn, your hat will be easy to clean. Follow the laundry care instructions on the yarn label and wash as directed. Lay flat to dry.

Embroidery Stitches

STRAIGHT STITCH

A simple, single stitch. Come up from wrong side of fabric at A and go down at B.

RUNNING STITCH

The Running Stitch is formed by a detached series of Straight Stitches. Make it by running the needle up and down the fabric at a regular distance. Come up at A, down at B, up at C, down at D, up at E, down at F, etc.

FRENCH KNOT

Bring needle up from wrong side at A. Place needle close to fabric and wrap yarn around needle 3 times. Push needle down at a point near A.

CHAIN STITCH EMBROIDERY

1. Bring needle up from wrong side at A. Put needle back in at A and out at B, but don't pull the needle completely through.

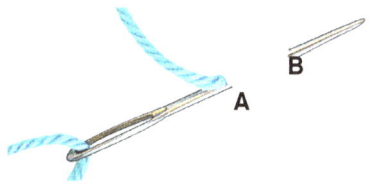

2. Wrap yarn around needle from left to right to form a loop.

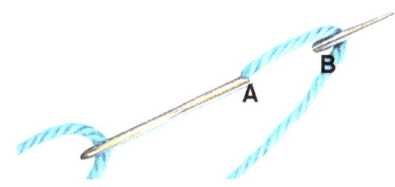

3. Pull needle out to tighten loop. First stitch is done.

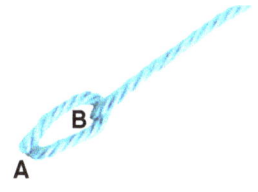

4. Put needle in at B and out at C. Repeat Steps 2 and 3 to complete 2nd stitch. Continue to make as many stitches as needed.

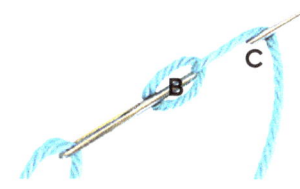

How to Measure your Gauge

Gauge is written as follows:

7 rnds of sc = 3" diameter circle

This means that when you've crocheted a 7-round flat circle of single crochet, the circle (or hexagon) you've created should have a 3" diameter. Most of these hats start with a flat circle. In that case, when you have crocheted the first 7 rounds, measure your work. If the measurement is 3", your gauge is correct. If the hat does not start with a flat circle, for example the Witch, Santa, Christmas Tree or Party Hat, crochet a gauge swatch with your yarn following the first 7 rounds of any ear-flap hat. To alter your gauge, adjust your crochet tension (tightness) or change to a larger or smaller crochet hook. It is very common for gauge to vary from person to person.

When laying flat, a completed earflap hat should measure 4" from top to bottom (excluding earflaps) and 6" across the center.

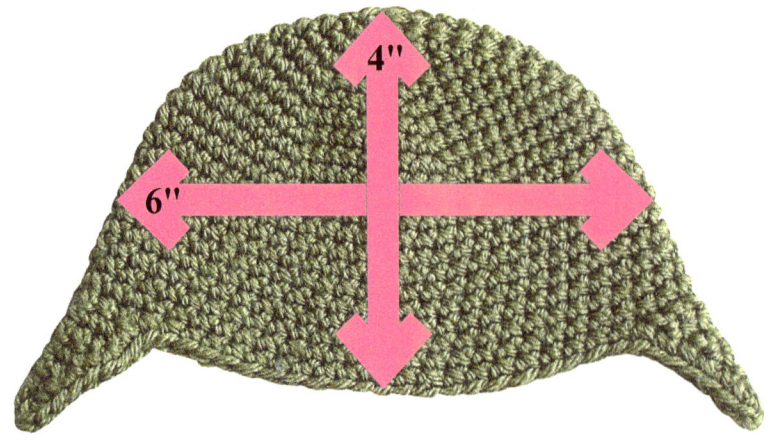

Abbreviations

Crochet patterns are written using abbreviations that save space and make the patterns easier to read.

The following abbreviations are used:

st	stitch
ch	chain
sc	single crochet
hdc	half double crochet
dc	double crochet
tr	triple crochet (also called treble crochet)
sl st	slip stitch
rnd	round
sc2tog	single crochet decrease
* *	repeat
( )	stitch count

How to Read a Pattern

Each round or row is written on a new line. Most rounds have a repeated section of instructions that are written between two asterisks *like this*. The instruction between the asterisks is to be repeated as many times as indicated before you move on to the next step. At the end of a round, the total number of stitches to be made in that round is indicated in parentheses (like this).

Let's look at a round from a hat:

Rnd 6: *sc in next 4 sts, 2 sc in next st* 6 times (36 sts).

This means:

Rnd 6	This is the 6th round of the pattern.
sc in next 4 sts	Make 1 single crochet stitch in each of the next 4 stitches
2 sc in next st	Make 2 single crochet stitches, both in the same stitch
6 times	Repeat everything between * and * 6 times.
(36 sts)	The round will have a total of 36 stitches.

So, following the instructions for Round 6, you will:

single crochet in the next 4 sts, 2 sc in the next st,
single crochet in the next 4 sts, 2 sc in the next st,
single crochet in the next 4 sts, 2 sc in the next st,
single crochet in the next 4 sts, 2 sc in the next st,
single crochet in the next 4 sts, 2 sc in the next st,
single crochet in the next 4 sts, 2 sc in the next st,

for a total of 36 stitches.

Valentine

SUPPLIES

Worsted weight yarn in pink (approx. 50 yards), white (approx. 20 yards), and red (approx 10 yards)

Size H/8 (5 mm) crochet hook or size needed to obtain gauge

Stitch marker

Yarn needle

GAUGE

7 rnds of sc = 3" diameter circle

HAT

With pink yarn, make a magic ring, ch 1.

Rnd 1: 6 sc in ring, pull ring closed tight (6 sts).

Rnd 2: 2 sc in each st around. Place marker for beginning of rnd and move marker up as each rnd is completed (12 sts).

Rnd 3: *sc in next st, 2 sc in next st* 6 times (18 sts).

Rnd 4: *sc in next 2 sts, 2 sc in next st* 6 times (24 sts).

Rnd 5: *sc in next 3 sts, 2 sc in next st* 6 times (30 sts).

Rnd 6: *sc in next 4 sts, 2 sc in next st* 6 times (36 sts).

Rnd 7: *sc in next 5 sts, 2 sc in next st* 6 times (42 sts).

Rnd 8: *sc in next 6 sts, 2 sc in next st* 6 times (48 sts).

Rnd 9: *sc in next 7 sts, 2 sc in next st* 6 times (54 sts).

Rnds 10-13: sc in each st around; change to white yarn in last st.

Rnd 14: sc in each st around; change to pink yarn in last st.

Rnds 15-16: sc in each st around; change to white yarn in last st.

Rnd 17: sc in each st around; change to pink yarn in last st.

Rnds 18-20: sc in each st around. Fasten off.

EAR FLAP (MAKE 2)

Mark position of Ear Flaps (see page 13). Note: A chain 1 at the beginning of a Row is for turning your work and does not count as a stitch.

Row 1: With pink yarn, attach yarn in 1st st with sc, sc in next 6 sts. Place marker for beginning of row and move marker up as each row is completed (7 sts).

Row 2: ch 1, turn, skip next st, sc in next 6 sts (6 sts).

Row 3: ch 1, turn, skip next st, sc in next 5 sts (5 sts).

Row 4: ch 1, turn, skip next st, sc in next 4 sts (4 sts).

Row 5: ch 1, turn, skip next st, sc in next 3 sts (3 sts).

Row 6: ch 1, turn, skip next st, sc in next 2 sts (2 sts).

Row 7: ch 1, turn, skip next st, sc in next st (1 st).

Fasten off. Weave in end.

EDGE TRIM

Using white yarn, attach yarn at center back of Hat with sc.

Rnd 1: *ch 3, sl st in 1st ch, sc in next 2 sts* around perimeter of Hat. Fasten off.

TWISTED CORD TIE (MAKE 2)

Cut three 24" strands of red yarn and three 24" strands of white yarn. Follow instructions on page 14.

HEART

With red yarn, chain 7 loosely.

Row 1: sc in 2nd chain from hook and in each remaining ch across (6 sts).

Rows 2-3: ch 1, turn, sc in each st across (6 sts).

Row 4: ch 1, turn, sc in 1st 3 sts (3 sts).

Rows 5-7: ch 1, turn, sc in each st across; change to white yarn in last st. (3 sts).

Rnd 8: continue to sc around entire heart. Note: When you get to the bottom stitch (the "point" of the heart), sc, ch 1, sc all in one stitch. When you get to the top "V" (indentation of the heart), sl st instead of sc.

Sl st in next st. Fasten off with long tail.

ASSEMBLY

Sew Heart to front of Hat. Weave in ends. ♦

Hearts Around

SUPPLIES

Worsted weight yarn in pink (approx. 60 yards) and dark red (approx. 30 yards)

Size H/8 (5 mm) crochet hook or size needed to obtain gauge

Lightweight cardboard

Stitch marker

Yarn needle

GAUGE

7 rnds of sc = 3" diameter circle

HAT

With pink yarn, make a magic ring, ch 1.

Rnd 1: 6 sc in ring, pull ring closed tight (6 sts).

Rnd 2: 2 sc in each st around. Place marker for beginning of rnd and move marker up as each rnd is completed (12 sts).

Rnd 3: *sc in next st, 2 sc in next st* 6 times (18 sts).

Rnd 4: *sc in next 2 sts, 2 sc in next st* 6 times (24 sts).

Rnd 5: *sc in next 3 sts, 2 sc in next st* 6 times (30 sts).

Rnd 6: *sc in next 4 sts, 2 sc in next st* 6 times (36 sts).

Rnd 7: *sc in next 5 sts, 2 sc in next st* 6 times (42 sts).

Rnd 8: *sc in next 6 sts, 2 sc in next st* 6 times (48 sts).

Rnd 9: *sc in next 7 sts, 2 sc in next st* 6 times (54 sts).

Rnds 10-20: sc in each st around. Fasten off.

EAR FLAP (MAKE 2)

Mark position of Ear Flaps (see page 13). Note: A chain 1 at the beginning of a Row is for turning your work and does not count as a stitch.

Row 1: With pink yarn, attach yarn in 1st st with sc, sc in next 6 sts. Place marker for beginning of row and move marker up as each row is completed (7 sts).

Row 2: ch 1, turn, skip next st, sc in next 6 sts (6 sts).

Row 3: ch 1, turn, skip next st, sc in next 5 sts (5 sts).

Row 4: ch 1, turn, skip next st, sc in next 4 sts (4 sts).

Row 5: ch 1, turn, skip next st, sc in next 3 sts (3 sts).

Row 6: ch 1, turn, skip next st, sc in next 2 sts (2 sts).

Row 7: ch 1, turn, skip next st, sc in next st (1 st).

Fasten off. Weave in end.

EDGE TRIM

Using red yarn, attach yarn at center back of Hat with sc.

Rnd 1: *5 sc in next st, skip next st, sl st in next st* around.

Fasten off.

TWISTED CORD TIE (MAKE 2)

Cut three 24" strands of red yarn and three 24" strands of pink yarn. Follow instructions on page 14.

SMALL POM POM (MAKE 2)

With red and pink yarn, follow instructions on page 15.

Note: These are 2-tone Pom Poms. Hold both colors together when wrapping yarn around cardboard ring.

SMALL HEART (MAKE 2)

With red yarn, chain 5 loosely.

Row 1: sc in 2nd chain from hook and in each remaining ch across (4 sts).

Row 2: ch 1, turn, sc in each st across (4 sts).

Row 3: ch 1, turn, sc in 1st 2 sts (2 sts).

26 Hearts Around

Rows 4-5: ch 1, turn, sc in each st across (2 sts).

Rnd 6: continue to sc around entire heart. Note: When you get to the top "V" (indentation of heart), sl st instead of sc. When you get to the bottom stitch (point of heart), sc, ch 1, sc all in one stitch.

Sl st in next st. Fasten off with long tail.

LARGE HEART (MAKE 2)

With red yarn, chain 7 loosely.

Row 1: sc in 2nd chain from hook and in each remaining ch across (6 sts).

Rows 2-3: ch 1, turn, sc in each st across (6 sts).

Row 4: ch 1, turn, sc in 1st 3 sts (3 sts).

Rows 5-7: ch 1, turn, sc in each st across (3 sts).

Rnd 8: continue to sc around entire heart. Note: When you get to the bottom stitch (point of heart), sc, ch 1, sc all in one stitch. When you get to the top "V" (indentation of heart), sl st instead of sc.

Sl st in next st. Fasten off with long tail.

ASSEMBLY

Sew Large Hearts at center front and center back of Hat. Sew Small Hearts at sides of Hat. Weave in ends. ♦

Shamrock

SUPPLIES

Worsted weight yarn in light green (approx. 60 yards) plus small amount of dark green

Size H/8 (5 mm) crochet hook or size needed to obtain gauge

Lightweight cardboard

Stitch marker

Yarn needle

GAUGE

7 rnds of sc = 3" diameter circle

HAT

With light green yarn, make a magic ring, ch 1.

Rnd 1: 6 sc in ring, pull ring closed tight (6 sts).

Rnd 2: 2 sc in each st around. Place marker for beginning of rnd and move marker up as each rnd is completed (12 sts).

Rnd 3: *sc in next st, 2 sc in next st* 6 times (18 sts).

Rnd 4: *sc in next 2 sts, 2 sc in next st* 6 times (24 sts).

Rnd 5: *sc in next 3 sts, 2 sc in next st* 6 times (30 sts).

Rnd 6: *sc in next 4 sts, 2 sc in next st* 6 times (36 sts).

Rnd 7: *sc in next 5 sts, 2 sc in next st* 6 times (42 sts).

Rnd 8: *sc in next 6 sts, 2 sc in next st* 6 times (48 sts).

Rnd 9: *sc in next 7 sts, 2 sc in next st* 6 times (54 sts).

Rnds 10-20: sc in each st around. Fasten off.

EAR FLAP (MAKE 2)

Mark position of Ear Flaps (see page 13). Note: A chain 1 at the beginning of a Row is for turning your work and does not count as a stitch.

Row 1: With light green yarn, attach yarn in 1st st with sc, sc in next 6 sts. Place marker for beginning of row and move marker up as each row is completed (7 sts).

Row 2: ch 1, turn, skip next st, sc in next 6 sts (6 sts).

Row 3: ch 1, turn, skip next st, sc in next 5 sts (5 sts).

Row 4: ch 1, turn, skip next st, sc in next 4 sts (4 sts).

Row 5: ch 1, turn, skip next st, sc in next 3 sts (3 sts).

Row 6: ch 1, turn, skip next st, sc in next 2 sts (2 sts).

Row 7: ch 1, turn, skip next st, sc in next st (1 st).

Fasten off. Weave in end.

EDGE TRIM

Rnd 1: Using dark green yarn, attach yarn at center back of Hat with sc. Sc in each st around perimeter of Hat making 3 sts at tip of each Ear Flap. Fasten off.

TWISTED CORD TIE (MAKE 2)

Cut three 24" strands of dark green yarn and three 24" strands of light green yarn. Follow instructions on page 14.

SMALL POM POM (MAKE 2)

With dark green yarn, follow instructions on page 15.

SHAMROCK

With dark green yarn, make a magic ring, ch 1.

Rnd 1: 6 sc in ring, pull ring closed tight (6 sts).

Rnd 2 (petals): Join with sl st to 1st sc, *ch 4, 3 tr in next sc on ring, ch 4, sl st in next sc on ring* 3 times.

Row 3 (stem): ch 6 (6 sts).

Row 4: turn, dc in 2nd ch from hook, sc in each remaining ch across (5 sts).

Sl st in next st. Fasten off with long tail.

ASSEMBLY

Sew Shamrock to Hat. Weave in ends. ♦

Top Hat

The **Top Hat** can be adapted for several holidays. Instructions are provided below for the **St. Patrick's Day** version. See photos on page 31 for the colors to use to make **Thanksgiving**, **New Year's** and **July 4th** versions.

SUPPLIES

Worsted weight yarn in green (approx. 70 yards) plus small amount of black and gold

Size H/8 (5 mm) crochet hook or size needed to obtain gauge

Stitch marker

Yarn needle

GAUGE

7 rnds of sc = 3" diameter circle

HAT

With green yarn, make a magic ring, ch 1.

Rnd 1: 6 sc in ring, pull ring closed tight (6 sts).

Rnd 2: 2 sc in each st around. Place marker for beginning of rnd and move marker up as each rnd is completed (12 sts).

Rnd 3: *sc in next st, 2 sc in next st* 6 times (18 sts).

Rnd 4: *sc in next 2 sts, 2 sc in next st* 6 times (24 sts).

Rnd 5: *sc in next 3 sts, 2 sc in next st* 6 times (30 sts).

Rnd 6: *sc in next 4 sts, 2 sc in next st* 6 times (36 sts).

Rnd 7: *sc in next 5 sts, 2 sc in next st* 6 times (42 sts).

Rnd 8: *sc in next 6 sts, 2 sc in next st* 6 times (48 sts).

Rnd 9: *sc in next 7 sts, 2 sc in next st* 6 times (54 sts).

Rnd 10: *sc in next 8 sts, 2 sc in next st* 6 times (60 sts).

Rnds 11-17: sc in each st around.

Rnd 18: *sc in next 4 sts, sc2tog* 10 times (50 sts).

Rnd 19: sc in each st around.

Rnd 20: *sc in next 3 sts, sc2tog* 10 times; change to black yarn in last st (40 sts).

Rnds 21-24: sc in each st around; change to green yarn in last st.

Rnd 25: *sc in next st, 2 sc in next st* 20 times (60 sts).

Rnd 26: *sc in next 9 sts, 2 sc in next st* 6 times (66 sts).

Rnds 27: *sc in next 10 sts, 2 sc in next st* 6 times (72 sts).

Rnd 28: *sc in next 11 sts, 2 sc in next st* 6 times (78 sts).

Rnd 29: sl st in each st around.

St st in next st. Fasten off.

ASSEMBLY

Using gold yarn, embroider buckle with chain stitch embroidery (see page 17). Weave in ends. ♦

St. Patrick's Day

Top Hat 31

Independence Day

The 4th of July Top Hat was crocheted in red yarn with a navy blue band. Sequin stars embellish the band.

Thanksgiving

The Pilgrim Top Hat was crocheted in brown yarn with an orange band. Gray yarn was used for the embroidered buckle.

New Year's Eve

The New Year's Top Hat was crocheted in solid pink. Purchased ribbon was used for the band.

Funky Bunny

SUPPLIES

Worsted weight yarn in lavender (approx. 45 yards), yellow (approx. 45 yards), pink (approx 45 yards) and green (approx 35 yards)

Size H/8 (5 mm) crochet hook or size needed to obtain gauge

Lightweight cardboard

2 pipe cleaners

Stitch marker

Yarn needle

GAUGE

7 rnds of sc = 3" diameter circle

HAT

With yellow yarn, make a magic ring, ch 1.

Rnd 1: 6 sc in ring, pull ring closed tight (6 sts).

Rnd 2: 2 sc in each st around. Place marker for beginning of rnd and move marker up as each rnd is completed (12 sts).

Rnd 3: *sc in next st, 2 sc in next st* 6 times (18 sts).

Rnd 4: *sc in next 2 sts, 2 sc in next st* 6 times; change to green yarn in last st (24 sts).

Rnd 5: *sc in next 3 sts, 2 sc in next st* 6 times (30 sts).

Rnd 6: *sc in next 4 sts, 2 sc in next st* 6 times (36 sts).

Rnd 7: *sc in next 5 sts, 2 sc in next st* 6 times (42 sts).

Rnd 8: *sc in next 6 sts, 2 sc in next st* 6 times; change to pink yarn in last st (48 sts).

Rnd 9: *sc in next 7 sts, 2 sc in next st* 6 times (54 sts).

Rnds 10-12: sc in each st around; change to lavender yarn in last st.

Rnds 13-16: sc in each st around; change to yellow yarn in last st.

Rnds 17-20: sc in each st around. Fasten off.

EAR FLAP (MAKE 2)

Mark position of Ear Flaps (see page 13). Note: A chain 1 at the beginning of a Row is for turning your work and does not count as a stitch.

Row 1: With yellow yarn, attach yarn in 1st st with sc, sc in next 6 sts. Place marker for beginning of row and move marker up as each row is completed (7 sts).

Row 2: ch 1, turn, skip next st, sc in next 6 sts (6 sts).

Row 3: ch 1, turn, skip next st, sc in next 5 sts (5 sts).

Row 4: ch 1, turn, skip next st, sc in next 4 sts (4 sts).

Row 5: ch 1, turn, skip next st, sc in next 3 sts (3 sts).

Row 6: ch 1, turn, skip next st, sc in next 2 sts (2 sts).

Row 7: ch 1, turn, skip next st, sc in next st (1 st).

Fasten off. Weave in end.

EDGE TRIM

Rnd 1: Using green yarn, attach yarn at center back of Hat with sc. Sc in each st around perimeter of Hat making 3 sts at tip of each Ear Flap. Fasten off.

TWISTED CORD TIE (MAKE 2)

Cut three 24" strands of pink yarn and three 24" strands of lavender yarn. Follow instructions on page 14.

SMALL POM POM (MAKE 2)

With lavender, yellow, green and pink yarn, follow instructions on page 15.

Note: These are multicolor Pom Poms. Hold all colors together when wrapping yarn around cardboard ring.

34 Funky Bunny

EAR (MAKE 2)

The front of each Ear is lavender and the back is yellow. Make 1 ear piece with lavender yarn and 1 ear piece with yellow yarn.

With lavender or yellow yarn, chain 5 loosely.

Row 1: sc in 2nd chain from hook and each st across (4 sts).

Row 2: ch 1, turn, 2 sc in next st, sc in next 2 sts, 2 sc in next st (6 sts).

Row 3: ch 1, turn, sc in each st across (6 sts).

Row 4: ch 1, turn, 2 sc in next st, sc in next 4 sts, 2 sc in next st (8 sts).

Rows 5-10: ch 1, turn, sc in each st across (8 sts).

Row 11: ch 1, turn, sc2tog, sc in next 4 sts, sc2tog (6 sts).

Row 12: ch 1, turn, sc in each st across (6 sts).

Row 13: ch 1, turn, sc2tog, sc in next 2 sts, sc2tog (4 sts).

Row 14: ch 1, turn, sc in each st across (4 sts).

Row 15: ch 1, turn, sc2tog twice (2 sts).

Row 16: ch 1, turn, sc2tog (1 st).

Fasten off. Weave in ends.

Place lavender and yellow pieces wrong sides together. With green yarn, sc pieces together around outer edge making 3 sts at each corner. Pause before pieces are completely crocheted together to insert pipe cleaner lengthwise into ear, cutting pipe cleaner to fit. Fasten off with long tail.

FLOWER

With pink yarn, follow instructions for Flower on page 36.

FLOWER CENTER

With green yarn, make a magic ring, ch 1.

Rnd 1: 4 sc in ring, pull ring closed tight (4 sts).

Sl st in next st. Fasten off with long tail.

ASSEMBLY

Sew Ears slightly cupped to top of Hat. Sew Flower to Hat. Sew Flower Center in place. Weave in ends. ♦

Easter Bonnet

SUPPLIES

Worsted weight yarn in white (approx. 55 yards) plus small amount of lavender, pink, green and yellow

Size H/8 (5 mm) crochet hook or size needed to obtain gauge

Stitch marker

Yarn needle

GAUGE

7 rnds of sc = 3" diameter circle

HAT

With white yarn, make a magic ring, ch 1.

Rnd 1: 6 sc in ring, pull ring closed tight (6 sts).

Rnd 2: 2 sc in each st around. Place marker for beginning of rnd and move marker up as each rnd is completed (12 sts).

Rnd 3: *sc in next st, 2 sc in next st* 6 times (18 sts).

Rnd 4: *sc in next 2 sts, 2 sc in next st* 6 times (24 sts).

Rnd 5: *sc in next 3 sts, 2 sc in next st* 6 times (30 sts).

Rnd 6: *sc in next 4 sts, 2 sc in next st* 6 times (36 sts).

Rnd 7: *sc in next 5 sts, 2 sc in next st* 6 times (42 sts).

Rnd 8: *sc in next 6 sts, 2 sc in next st* 6 times (48 sts).

Rnd 9: *sc in next 7 sts, 2 sc in next st* 6 times (54 sts).

Rnds 10-20: sc in each st around. Fasten off.

EAR FLAP (MAKE 2)

Mark position of Ear Flaps (see page 13). Note: A chain 1 at the beginning of a Row is for turning your work and does not count as a stitch.

Row 1: With white yarn, attach yarn in 1st st with sc, sc in next 6 sts. Place marker for beginning of row and move marker up as each row is completed (7 sts).

Row 2: ch 1, turn, skip next st, sc in next 6 sts (6 sts).

Row 3: ch 1, turn, skip next st, sc in next 5 sts (5 sts).

Row 4: ch 1, turn, skip next st, sc in next 4 sts (4 sts).

Row 5: ch 1, turn, skip next st, sc in next 3 sts (3 sts).

Row 6: ch 1, turn, skip next st, sc in next 2 sts (2 sts).

Row 7: ch 1, turn, skip next st, sc in next st (1 st).

Fasten off. Weave in end.

EDGE TRIM

Rnd 1: Using yellow yarn, attach yarn at center back of Hat with sc. Sc in each st around perimeter of Hat making 3 sts at tip of each Ear Flap. Fasten off.

TWISTED CORD TIE (MAKE 2)

Cut three 24" strands of yellow yarn and three 24" strands of green yarn. Follow instructions on page 14.

FLOWER (MAKE 2)

Make 1 with pink yarn and 1 with lavender yarn.

With desired color of yarn, ch 25 loosely.

Row 1: sc in 2nd ch from hook, *ch 2, skip 1 ch, sc in next ch* across.

Note: This creates 12 spaces into which you will crochet the petals. See Figure A.

Row 2: ch 1, turn, *sl st in next space, ch 1, 5 dc in same space, ch 1, sl st in same space* across. See Figure B.

Fasten off with long tail. Coil strip of petals into a flower shape with lower layer of petals extending beyond upper layer. Thread long tail into yarn needle and stitch through all layers at several points to secure petals into a pretty flower.

FLOWER CENTER (MAKE 2)

With yellow yarn, make a magic ring, ch 1.

Rnd 1: 4 sc in ring, pull ring closed tight (4 sts).

Sl st in next st. Fasten off with long tail.

LEAF (MAKE 5)

The Leaf is worked around a foundation chain.

With green yarn, ch 8 loosely.

Rnd 1: sc in 2nd ch from hook, hdc in next ch, dc in next 3 ch, hdc in next ch, 3 sc in end ch, hdc in next ch, dc in next 3 ch, hdc in next ch, sc in next ch, sl st in 1st ch. Place marker at beginning of rnd. (16 sts).

Fasten off with long tail.

ASSEMBLY

Sew Flowers to Hat. Sew Flower Centers in place. Tuck Leaves under Flowers and sew to Hat. Weave in ends. ♦

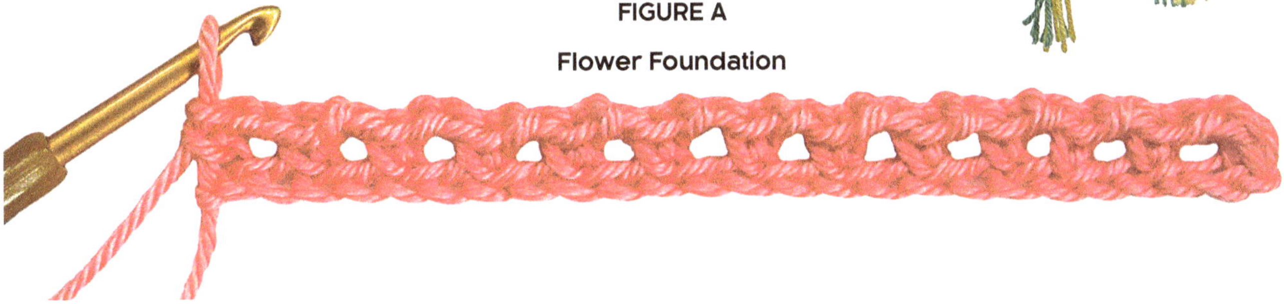

FIGURE A
Flower Foundation

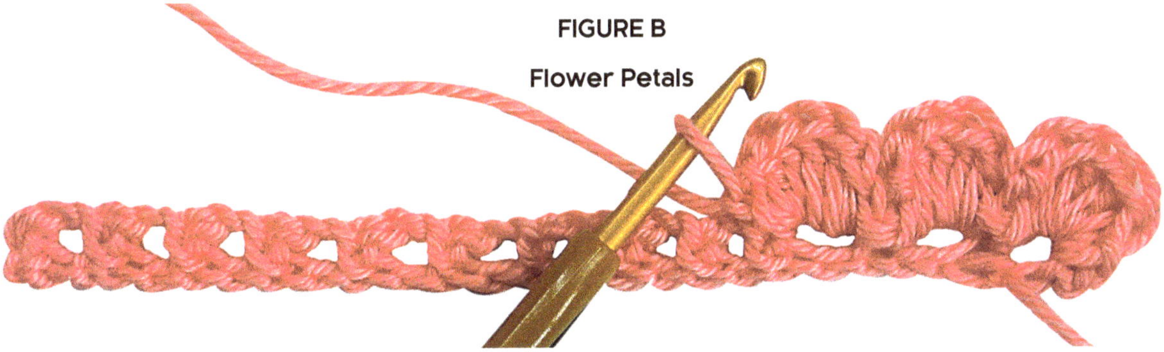

FIGURE B
Flower Petals

Easter Chick

SUPPLIES

Worsted weight yarn in aqua (approx. 70 yards) plus small amount of yellow

Size H/8 (5 mm) crochet hook or size needed to obtain gauge

2 black buttons, 3/8" diameter

2 yellow buttons, 5/8" diameter

Sewing needle and thread

Lightweight cardboard

Stitch marker

Yarn needle

GAUGE

7 rnds of sc = 3" diameter circle

HAT

With aqua yarn, make a magic ring, ch 1.

Rnd 1: 6 sc in ring, pull ring closed tight (6 sts).

Rnd 2: 2 sc in each st around. Place marker for beginning of rnd and move marker up as each rnd is completed (12 sts).

Rnd 3: *sc in next st, 2 sc in next st* 6 times (18 sts).

Rnd 4: *sc in next 2 sts, 2 sc in next st* 6 times (24 sts).

Rnd 5: *sc in next 3 sts, 2 sc in next st* 6 times (30 sts).

Rnd 6: *sc in next 4 sts, 2 sc in next st* 6 times (36 sts).

Rnd 7: *sc in next 5 sts, 2 sc in next st* 6 times (42 sts).

Rnd 8: *sc in next 6 sts, 2 sc in next st* 6 times (48 sts).

Rnd 9: *sc in next 7 sts, 2 sc in next st* 6 times (54 sts).

Rnds 10-20: sc in each st around. Fasten off.

EAR FLAP (MAKE 2)

Mark position of Ear Flaps (see page 13). Note: A chain 1 at the beginning of a Row is for turning your work and does not count as a stitch.

Row 1: With aqua yarn, attach yarn in 1st st with sc, sc in next 6 sts. Place marker for beginning of row and move marker up as each row is completed (7 sts).

Row 2: ch 1, turn, skip next st, sc in next 6 sts (6 sts).

Row 3: ch 1, turn, skip next st, sc in next 5 sts (5 sts).

Row 4: ch 1, turn, skip next st, sc in next 4 sts (4 sts).

Row 5: ch 1, turn, skip next st, sc in next 3 sts (3 sts).

Row 6: ch 1, turn, skip next st, sc in next 2 sts (2 sts).

Row 7: ch 1, turn, skip next st, sc in next st (1 st).

Fasten off. Weave in end.

EDGE TRIM

Using aqua yarn, attach yarn at center back of Hat with sc.

Rnd 1: *4 sc in next st, skip next st, sl st in next st* around.

Fasten off.

TWISTED CORD TIE (MAKE 2)

Cut six 24" strands of aqua yarn. Follow instructions on page 14.

SMALL POM POM (MAKE 2)

With aqua yarn, follow instructions on page 15.

BEAK

With yellow yarn, ch 2 loosely.

Row 1: sc in 2nd chain from hook (1 st).

Row 2: ch 1, turn, 2 sc in next st (2 sts).

Row 3: ch 1, turn, sc in next st, 2 sc in next st (3 sts).

Row 4: ch 1, turn, sc in each st across (3 sts).

40 Easter Chick

Row 5: ch 1, turn, sc2tog, sc in next st (2 sts).

Row 6: ch 1, turn, sc2tog (1st).

Rnd 7: sc in each st around entire perimeter making 3 sts in same st at each point.

Sl st in next st. Fasten off with long tail.

TUFT

Cut four 6-inch strands of aqua yarn. Lay strands together side by side and attach to top of Hat using Fringe technique (see page 16). Trim ends even.

ASSEMBLY

Fold Beak in half and sew to Hat. Stack black buttons on yellow buttons and sew in place for eyes. Weave in ends. ♦

Stars & Stripes

SUPPLIES

Worsted weight yarn in red, white and navy blue (approx. 30 yards each)

Size H/8 (5 mm) crochet hook or size needed to obtain gauge

8 white star sequins or buttons, 1/2" tall

8 white seed beads (if sequin stars are used)

Sewing needle and thread

Small piece of cardboard

Stitch marker

Yarn needle

GAUGE

7 rnds of sc = 3" diameter circle

HAT

With red yarn, make a magic ring, ch 1.

Rnd 1: 6 sc in ring, pull ring closed tight (6 sts).

Rnd 2: 2 sc in each st around; change to white yarn in last st. Place marker for beginning of rnd and move marker up as each rnd is completed (12 sts).

Rnd 3: *sc in next st, 2 sc in next st* 6 times (18 sts).

Rnd 4: *sc in next 2 sts, 2 sc in next st* 6 times; change to red yarn in last st (24 sts).

Rnd 5: *sc in next 3 sts, 2 sc in next st* 6 times (30 sts).

Rnd 6: *sc in next 4 sts, 2 sc in next st* 6 times; change to white yarn in last st (36 sts).

Rnd 7: *sc in next 5 sts, 2 sc in next st* 6 times (42 sts).

Rnd 8: *sc in next 6 sts, 2 sc in next st* 6 times; change to red yarn in last st (48 sts).

Rnd 9: *sc in next 7 sts, 2 sc in next st* 6 times (54 sts).

Rnd 10: sc in each st around; change to white yarn in last st.

Rnds 11-12: sc in each st around; change to red yarn in last st.

Rnds 13-14: sc in each st around; change to white yarn in last st.

Rnds 15-16: sc in each st around; change to blue yarn in last st.

Rnds 17-20: sc in each st around.

Fasten off.

EAR FLAP (MAKE 2)

Mark position of Ear Flaps (see page 13). Note: A chain 1 at the beginning of a Row is for turning your work and does not count as a stitch.

Row 1: With blue yarn, attach yarn in 1st st with sc, sc in next 6 sts. Place marker for beginning of row and move marker up as each row is completed (7 sts).

Row 2: ch 1, turn, skip next st, sc in next 6 sts (6 sts).

Row 3: ch 1, turn, skip next st, sc in next 5 sts (5 sts).

Row 4: ch 1, turn, skip next st, sc in next 4 sts (4 sts).

Row 5: ch 1, turn, skip next st, sc in next 3 sts (3 sts).

Row 6: ch 1, turn, skip next st, sc in next 2 sts (2 sts).

Row 7: ch 1, turn, skip next st, sc in next st (1 st).

Fasten off. Weave in end.

EDGE TRIM

Rnd 1: Using red yarn, attach yarn at center back of Hat with sc. Sc in each st around perimeter of Hat making 3 sts at tip of each Ear Flap. Fasten off.

TWISTED CORD TIE (MAKE 2)

Cut three 24" strands of red yarn and three 24" strands of white yarn. Follow instructions on page 14.

Stars & Stripes

FIREWORKS POM POM (MAKE 2)

Note: These are multi-color Pom Poms. Hold all 3 colors together when wrapping yarn around cardboard.

Cut a 4"x4" square of cardboard. Wrap red, white and blue yarn around cardboard 20 times. Carefully slide yarn off cardboard. Using a scrap of yarn, tie bundle together tightly around the middle. Wrap tails of tie to opposite side and tie again. Cut loops open.

ASSEMBLY

Place Pom Poms in position on Hat and pull long tails through to wrong side. Tie Pom Poms to Hat. Sew star buttons or sequins on blue band. If sequins are used, attach as follows: bring needle and thread up through Hat from wrong side, push needle through hole in sequin, insert seed bead on needle, then push needle back down through hole in sequin to wrong side of Hat. Weave in ends. ♦

Pumpkin

SUPPLIES

Worsted weight yarn in orange (approx. 65 yards) plus small amount of brown, green and black

Size H/8 (5 mm) crochet hook or size needed to obtain gauge

Disappearing ink marking pen

Stuffing

Stitch marker

Yarn needle

GAUGE

7 rnds of sc = 3" diameter circle

HAT

With orange yarn, make a magic ring, ch 1.

Rnd 1: 6 sc in ring, pull ring closed tight (6 sts).

Rnd 2: 2 sc in each st around. Place marker for beginning of rnd and move marker up as each rnd is completed (12 sts).

Rnd 3: *sc in next st, 2 sc in next st* 6 times (18 sts).

Rnd 4: *sc in next 2 sts, 2 sc in next st* 6 times (24 sts).

Rnd 5: *sc in next 3 sts, 2 sc in next st* 6 times (30 sts).

Rnd 6: *sc in next 4 sts, 2 sc in next st* 6 times (36 sts).

Rnd 7: *sc in next 5 sts, 2 sc in next st* 6 times (42 sts).

Rnd 8: *sc in next 6 sts, 2 sc in next st* 6 times (48 sts).

Rnd 9: *sc in next 7 sts, 2 sc in next st* 6 times (54 sts).

Rnds 10-20: sc in each st around. Fasten off.

EAR FLAP (MAKE 2)

Mark position of Ear Flaps (see page 13). Note: A chain 1 at the beginning of a Row is for turning your work and does not count as a stitch.

Row 1: With orange yarn, attach yarn in 1st st with sc, sc in next 6 sts. Place marker for beginning of row and move marker up as each row is completed (7 sts).

Row 2: ch 1, turn, skip next st, sc in next 6 sts (6 sts).

Row 3: ch 1, turn, skip next st, sc in next 5 sts (5 sts).

Row 4: ch 1, turn, skip next st, sc in next 4 sts (4 sts).

Row 5: ch 1, turn, skip next st, sc in next 3 sts (3 sts).

Row 6: ch 1, turn, skip next st, sc in next 2 sts (2 sts).

Row 7: ch 1, turn, skip next st, sc in next st (1 st).

Fasten off. Weave in end.

EDGE TRIM

Rnd 1: Using orange yarn, attach yarn at center back of Hat with sc. Sc in each st around perimeter of Hat making 3 sts at tip of each Ear Flap. Fasten off.

TWISTED CORD TIE (MAKE 2)

Cut six 24" strands of green yarn. Follow instructions on page 14.

EYE (MAKE 2)

With black yarn, ch 5.

Row 1: starting in 2nd ch from hook, sc2tog twice (2 sts).

Row 2: ch 1, turn, sc in each st across (2 sts).

Row 3: ch 1, turn, sc2tog (1 st).

Fasten off with long tail. Pinch tips into sharp points.

STEM

With brown yarn, make a magic ring, ch 1.

Rnd 1: 4 sc in ring, pull ring closed tight (4 sts).

Rnd 2: *sc in next st, 2 sc in next st* 2 times. Place marker for beginning of rnd and move marker up as each rnd is completed (6 sts).

Rnd 3: sc in each st around.

Pumpkin

Rnd 4: *sc in next 2 sts, 2 sc in next st* 2 times (8 sts).

Rnd 5: sc in next st, sl st in next 2 sts, sc in next 5 sts (8 sts).

Rnd 6: sc in next st, sl st in next 2 sts, 2 sc in next st, sc in next 3 sts, 2 sc in next st (10 sts).

Rnd 7: sc in next st, sl st in next 2 sts, sc in next 7 sts (10 sts).

Rnd 8: sc in each st around.

Rnd 9: *sc in next 4 sts, 2 sc in next st* 2 times (12 sts).

Rnd 10: sc in each st around.

Sl st in next st. Fasten off with long tail.

LEAF

With green yarn, make a magic ring, ch 1.

Rnd 1: 8 sc in ring, pull ring closed tight (8 sts).

Rnd 2: 2 sc in each st around (16 sts).

Rnd 3: *5 sc in next st, skip next st, sl st in next st * around.

Fasten off with long tail.

TENDRIL

With green yarn, ch 20 loosely.

Row 1: sc in 2nd ch from hook and in each ch across (19 sts).

Fasten off. Curl with fingers into a tight spiral.

ASSEMBLY

Mark Mouth using Template (see page 81: To mark, punch holes in points of Template, hold in position on Hat and dot with disappearing ink marking pen in the holes. Embroider Mouth with a double strand of black yarn. Sew Eyes to Hat. Stuff Stem and sew to top of Hat. Sew Leaf and Tendril against Stem. Weave in ends. ♦

Leaf

Witch

SUPPLIES

Worsted weight yarn in purple (approx. 75 yards) plus small amount of green

Size H/8 (5 mm) crochet hook

Stitch marker

Yarn needle

GAUGE

7 rnds of sc = 3" diameter circle

HAT

With purple yarn, make a magic ring, ch 1.

Rnd 1: 6 sc in ring, pull ring closed tight (6 sts).

Rnd 2: 2 sc in each st around. Place marker for beginning of rnd and move marker up as each rnd is completed (12 sts).

Rnds 3-4: sc in each st around.

Rnd 5: *sc in next st, 2 sc in next st* 6 times (18 sts).

Rnds 6-7: sc in each st around.

Rnd 8: *sc in next 2 sts, 2 sc in next st* 6 times (24 sts).

Rnds 9-11: sc in each st around.

Rnd 12: *sc in next 3 sts, 2 sc in next st* 6 times (30 sts).

Rnds 13-15: sc in each st around.

Rnd 16: *sc in next 4 sts, 2 sc in next st* 6 times (36 sts).

Rnds 17-19: sc in each st around.

Rnd 20: *sc in next 5 sts, 2 sc in next st* 6 times (42 sts).

Rnds 21-24: sc in each st around.

Rnd 25: *sc in next 6 sts, 2 sc in next st* 6 times; fasten on with green yarn in last st (48 sts).

Rnds 26-29: sc in each st around; fasten on with purple yarn in last st.

Rnd 30: *sc in next 7 sts, 2 sc in next st* 6 times (54 sts).

Rnd 31: *sc in next 8 sts, 2 sc in next st* 6 times (60 sts).

Rnd 32: *sc in next 9 sts, 2 sc in next st* 6 times (66 sts).

Rnd 33: *sc in next 10 sts, 2 sc in next st* 6 times (72 sts).

Rnd 34: *sc in next 11 sts, 2 sc in next st* 6 times (78 sts).

Rnd 35: *sc in next 12 sts, 2 sc in next st* 6 times (84 sts).

Sl st in next st. Fasten off.

BOW

With green yarn, ch 9 loosely.

Row 1: sc in 2nd chain from hook and in each remaining ch across (8 sts).

Rows 2-3: ch 1, turn, sc in each st across (8 sts).

Rnd 4: sc in each st around next 3 sides. Join with sl st to next st. Fasten off.

Weave ends into wrong side. With a scrap of yarn, tie tightly across center of rectangle. Wrap 1 end around center several times to make a pretty pinched middle. Knot ends together leaving long tails.

ASSEMBLY

Place Bow in position on Hat and pull long tails through to wrong side. Tie Bow to Hat. Weave in ends.

♦

Black Cat

SUPPLIES

Worsted weight yarn in black (approx. 75 yards) plus small amount of orange and white

Size H/8 (5 mm) crochet hook or size needed to obtain gauge

2 yellow buttons, 5/8" diameter

Sewing needle and thread

Lightweight cardboard

Stitch marker

Yarn needle

GAUGE

7 rnds of sc = 3" diameter circle

HAT

With black yarn, make a magic ring, ch 1.

Rnd 1: 6 sc in ring, pull ring closed tight (6 sts).

Rnd 2: 2 sc in each st around. Place marker for beginning of rnd and move marker up as each rnd is completed (12 sts).

Rnd 3: *sc in next st, 2 sc in next st* 6 times (18 sts).

Rnd 4: *sc in next 2 sts, 2 sc in next st* 6 times (24 sts).

Rnd 5: *sc in next 3 sts, 2 sc in next st* 6 times (30 sts).

Rnd 6: *sc in next 4 sts, 2 sc in next st* 6 times (36 sts).

Rnd 7: *sc in next 5 sts, 2 sc in next st* 6 times (42 sts).

Rnd 8: *sc in next 6 sts, 2 sc in next st* 6 times (48 sts).

Rnd 9: *sc in next 7 sts, 2 sc in next st* 6 times (54 sts).

Rnds 10-20: sc in each st around.

Fasten off.

EAR FLAP (MAKE 2)

Mark position of Ear Flaps (see page 13). Note: A chain 1 at the beginning of a Row is for turning your work and does not count as a stitch.

Row 1: With black yarn, attach yarn in 1st st with sc, sc in next 6 sts. Place marker for beginning of row and move marker up as each row is completed (7 sts).

Row 2: ch 1, turn, skip next st, sc in next 6 sts (6 sts).

Row 3: ch 1, turn, skip next st, sc in next 5 sts (5 sts).

Row 4: ch 1, turn, skip next st, sc in next 4 sts (4 sts).

Row 5: ch 1, turn, skip next st, sc in next 3 sts (3 sts).

Row 6: ch 1, turn, skip next st, sc in next 2 sts (2 sts).

Row 7: ch 1, turn, skip next st, sc in next st (1 st).

Fasten off. Weave in end.

EDGE TRIM

Rnd 1: Using black yarn, attach yarn at center back of Hat with sc. Sc in each st around perimeter of Hat making 3 sts at tip of each Ear Flap. Fasten off.

TWISTED CORD TIE (MAKE 2)

Cut three 24" strands of black yarn and three 24" strands of orange yarn. Follow instructions on page 14.

SMALL POM POM (MAKE 2)

With black and orange yarn, follow instructions on page 15.

Note: These are 2-tone Pom Poms. Hold both colors together when wrapping yarn around cardboard ring.

EAR (MAKE 2)

The Ear is orange on front and black on back. Make 1 with orange yarn and 1 with black yarn.

With orange or black yarn, chain 7 loosely.

Row 1: sc in 2nd chain from hook and each st across (6 sts).

Rows 2-3: ch 1, turn, sc in each st across (6 sts).

Row 4: ch 1, turn, sc2tog, sc in next 2 sts, sc2tog (4 sts).

Row 5: ch 1, turn, sc in each st across (4 sts).

Row 6: ch 1, turn, sc2tog twice (2 sts).

Row 7: ch 1, turn, sc in each st across (2 sts).

Row 8: ch 1, turn, sc2tog (1 st).

Fasten off. Weave in ends, weaving over any holes made by decreases.

Place orange and black pieces wrong sides together. With black yarn, sc pieces together along outer edge making 3 sts at each corner. Fasten off with long tail.

NOSE

With orange yarn, ch 5.

Row 1: starting in 2nd ch from hook, sc2tog twice (2 sts).

Row 2: ch 1, turn, sc2tog (1 st).

Fasten off with long tail. Pinch tips into sharp points.

ASSEMBLY

Sew Ears slightly cupped to Hat. Sew Nose to Hat. With white yarn, embroider whiskers by making 1 long stitch for each whisker. Sew buttons to Hat for eyes. Weave in ends. ♦

Devil

SUPPLIES

Worsted weight yarn in red (approx. 60 yards) plus small amount of black

Size H/8 (5 mm) crochet hook or size needed to obtain gauge

Stuffing

Stitch marker

Yarn needle

GAUGE

7 rnds of sc = 3" diameter circle

HAT

With red yarn, make a magic ring, ch 1.

Rnd 1: 6 sc in ring, pull ring closed tight (6 sts).

Rnd 2: 2 sc in each st around. Place marker for beginning of rnd and move marker up as each rnd is completed (12 sts).

Rnd 3: *sc in next st, 2 sc in next st* 6 times (18 sts).

Rnd 4: *sc in next 2 sts, 2 sc in next st* 6 times (24 sts).

Rnd 5: *sc in next 3 sts, 2 sc in next st* 6 times (30 sts).

Rnd 6: *sc in next 4 sts, 2 sc in next st* 6 times (36 sts).

Rnd 7: *sc in next 5 sts, 2 sc in next st* 6 times (42 sts).

Rnd 8: *sc in next 6 sts, 2 sc in next st* 6 times (48 sts).

Rnd 9: *sc in next 7 sts, 2 sc in next st* 6 times (54 sts).

Rnds 10-20: sc in each st around.

Fasten off.

EAR FLAP (MAKE 2)

Mark position of Ear Flaps (see page 13). Note: A chain 1 at the beginning of a Row is for turning your work and does not count as a stitch.

Row 1: With red yarn, attach yarn in 1st st with sc, sc in next 6 sts. Place marker for beginning of row and move marker up as each row is completed (7 sts).

Row 2: ch 1, turn, skip next st, sc in next 6 sts (6 sts).

Row 3: ch 1, turn, skip next st, sc in next 5 sts (5 sts).

Row 4: ch 1, turn, skip next st, sc in next 4 sts (4 sts).

Row 5: ch 1, turn, skip next st, sc in next 3 sts (3 sts).

Row 6: ch 1, turn, skip next st, sc in next 2 sts (2 sts).

Row 7: ch 1, turn, skip next st, sc in next st (1 st).

Fasten off. Weave in end.

EDGE TRIM

Mark stitch at center front of Hat with stitch marker.

Rnd 1: Using black yarn, attach yarn at center back of Hat with sc. Sc in each st around perimeter of Hat making 3 sc in st at tip of each Ear Flap and 3 sc in st at center front. Fasten off.

TWISTED CORD TIE (MAKE 2)

Cut six 24" strands of red yarn. Follow instructions on page 14.

HORN (MAKE 2)

With black yarn, make a magic ring, ch 1.

Rnd 1: 4 sc in ring, pull ring closed tight (4 sts).

Rnd 2: *sc in next st, 2 sc in next st* 2 times. Place marker for beginning of rnd and move marker up as each rnd is completed (6 sts).

Rnd 3: sc in each st around.

Rnd 4: *sc in next 2 sts, 2 sc in next st* 2 times (8 sts).

Rnd 5: sc in next st, sl st in next 2 sts, sc in next 5 sts (8 sts).

Rnd 6: sc in next st, sl st in next 2 sts, 2 sc in next st, sc in next 3 sts, 2 sc in next st (10 sts).

54 Devil

Rnd 7: sc in next st, sl st in next 2 sts, sc in next 7 sts (10 sts).

Rnd 8: *sc in next 4 sts, 2 sc in next st* 2 times (12 sts).

Sl st in next st. Fasten off with long tail.

TRIANGLE (MAKE 2)

With black yarn, make magic ring, ch 1.

Rnd 1: 4 sc in ring, pull ring closed tight (4 sts).

Rnd 2: *sc in next st, 2 sc in next st* 2 times. Place marker for beginning of rnd and move marker up as each rnd is completed (6 sts).

Rnd 3: *sc in next 2 sts, 2 sc in next st* 2 times (8 sts).

Rnd 4: *sc in next 3 sts, 2 sc in next st* 2 times (10 sts).

Rnd 5: *sc in next 4 sts, 2 sc in next st* 2 times (12 sts).

Rnd 6: *sc in next 5 sts, 2 sc in next st* 2 times (14 sts).

Sl st in next st. Fasten off with long tail.

ASSEMBLY

Trim fringe on Twisted Cord Ties close to knots and insert ends in Triangles. Sew Triangles closed. Stuff Horns and sew to top of Hat. Weave in ends. ♦

Turkey

SUPPLIES

Worsted weight yarn in brown (approx. 50 yards) plus small amount of orange, yellow and red

Size H/8 (5 mm) crochet hook or size needed to obtain gauge

2 black buttons, 3/8" diameter

2 white buttons, 5/8" diameter

Sewing needle and thread

Stitch marker

Yarn needle

GAUGE

7 rnds of sc = 3" diameter circle

HAT

With brown yarn, make a magic ring, ch 1.

Rnd 1: 6 sc in ring, pull ring closed tight (6 sts).

Rnd 2: 2 sc in each st around. Place marker for beginning of rnd and move marker up as each rnd is completed (12 sts).

Rnd 3: *sc in next st, 2 sc in next st* 6 times (18 sts).

Rnd 4: *sc in next 2 sts, 2 sc in next st* 6 times (24 sts).

Rnd 5: *sc in next 3 sts, 2 sc in next st* 6 times (30 sts).

Rnd 6: *sc in next 4 sts, 2 sc in next st* 6 times (36 sts).

Rnd 7: *sc in next 5 sts, 2 sc in next st* 6 times (42 sts).

Rnd 8: *sc in next 6 sts, 2 sc in next st* 6 times (48 sts).

Rnd 9: *sc in next 7 sts, 2 sc in next st* 6 times (54 sts).

Rnds 10-20: sc in each st around.

Fasten off.

EAR FLAP (MAKE 2)

Mark position of Ear Flaps (see page 13). Note: A chain 1 at the beginning of a Row is for turning your work and does not count as a stitch.

Row 1: With brown yarn, attach yarn in 1st st with sc, sc in next 6 sts. Place marker for beginning of row and move marker up as each row is completed (7 sts).

Row 2: ch 1, turn, skip next st, sc in next 6 sts (6 sts).

Row 3: ch 1, turn, skip next st, sc in next 5 sts (5 sts).

Row 4: ch 1, turn, skip next st, sc in next 4 sts (4 sts).

Row 5: ch 1, turn, skip next st, sc in next 3 sts (3 sts).

Row 6: ch 1, turn, skip next st, sc in next 2 sts (2 sts).

Row 7: ch 1, turn, skip next st, sc in next st (1 st).

Fasten off. Weave in end.

EDGE TRIM

Rnd 1: Using orange yarn, attach yarn at center back of Hat with sc. Sc in each st around perimeter of Hat making 3 sts at tip of each Ear Flap. Fasten off.

TWISTED CORD TIE (MAKE 2)

Cut three 24" strands of orange yarn and three 24" strands of red yarn. Follow instructions on page 14.

FEATHER (MAKE 10)

The Feather is worked around a foundation chain. Each final feather is made from 2 pieces that are sewn together. Make 2 feather pieces from red yarn, 4 from yellow yarn and 4 from orange yarn.

With desired color of yarn, ch 11 loosely.

Rnd 1: sc in 2nd ch from hook, hdc in next ch, dc in next 6 ch, hdc in next ch, 3 sc in end ch, hdc in next ch, dc in next 6 ch, hdc in next ch, sc in next ch, sl st in 1st ch (22 sts).

Fasten off with long tail.

Divide feathers into same-color sets of 2. Sew each set together back to back. Pinch tips into nice points. Weave in ends.

BEAK

With yellow yarn, ch 5.

Row 1: starting in 2nd ch from hook, sc2tog twice (2 sts).

Row 2: ch 1, turn, sc in each st across (2 sts).

Row 3: ch 1, turn, sc2tog (1 st).

Fasten off with long tail. Pinch corners into sharp points.

ASSEMBLY

Flatten hat with center front and center back aligned. Thread yarn needle with contrasting yarn and baste along creaseline with running sts. Sew feathers to Hat 1/2" behind basted guideline. Remove basting sts. Sew Beak to Hat. Stack black buttons on white buttons and sew in place for eyes. Weave in ends. ♦

SUPPLIES

Worsted weight yarn in red (approx. 60 yards) and white (approx. 30 yards)

Size H/8 (5 mm) crochet hook

Lightweight cardboard

Stiff hair brush

Stitch marker

Yarn needle

GAUGE

7 rnds of sc = 3" diameter circle

HAT

With red yarn, make a magic ring, ch 1.

Rnd 1: 6 sc in ring, pull ring closed tight (6 sts).

Rnd 2: 2 sc in each st around. Place marker for beginning of rnd and move marker up as each rnd is completed (12 sts).

Rnds 3-4: sc in each st around.

Rnd 5: *sc in next st, 2 sc in next st* 6 times (18 sts).

Rnds 6-7: sc in each st around.

Rnd 8: *sc in next 2 sts, 2 sc in next st* 6 times (24 sts).

Rnds 9-11: sc in each st around.

Rnd 12: *sc in next 3 sts, 2 sc in next st* 6 times (30 sts).

Rnds 13-15: sc in each st around.

Rnd 16: *sc in next 4 sts, 2 sc in next st* 6 times (36 sts).

Rnds 17-19: sc in each st around.

Rnd 20: *sc in next 5 sts, 2 sc in next st* 6 times (42 sts).

Rnds 21-24: sc in each st around.

Rnd 25: *sc in next 6 sts, 2 sc in next st* 6 times (48 sts).

Rnds 26-29: sc in each st around.

Rnd 30: *sc in next 7 sts, 2 sc in next st* 6 times (54 sts).

Rnds 31-35: sc in each st around; change to white yarn in last st.

Rnds 36-45: sc in each st around.

Sl st in last st. Fasten off.

SMALL POM POM

With white yarn, use Small Pom Pom template but follow instructions for Medium and Large Pom Poms on page 15.

ASSEMBLY

Place Pom Pom at tip of Hat and pull long tails through to wrong side. Tie Pom Pom to Hat. Roll up brim. Brush brim to make it fuzzier. Weave in ends. ♦

SUPPLIES

Worsted weight yarn in tan (approx. 70 yards) plus small amount of brown and red

Size H/8 (5 mm) crochet hook or size needed to obtain gauge

2 black buttons, 1/2" diameter

2 white buttons, 3/4" diameter

Sewing needle & thread

Stuffing

Wooden spoon

Stitch marker

Yarn needle

GAUGE

7 rnds of sc = 3" diameter circle

HAT

With tan yarn, make a magic ring, ch 1.

Rnd 1: 6 sc in ring, pull ring closed tight (6 sts).

Rnd 2: 2 sc in each st around. Place marker for beginning of rnd and move marker up as each rnd is completed (12 sts).

Rnd 3: *sc in next st, 2 sc in next st* 6 times (18 sts).

Rnd 4: *sc in next 2 sts, 2 sc in next st* 6 times (24 sts).

Rnd 5: *sc in next 3 sts, 2 sc in next st* 6 times (30 sts).

Rnd 6: *sc in next 4 sts, 2 sc in next st* 6 times (36 sts).

Rnd 7: *sc in next 5 sts, 2 sc in next st* 6 times (42 sts).

Rnd 8: *sc in next 6 sts, 2 sc in next st* 6 times (48 sts).

Rnd 9: *sc in next 7 sts, 2 sc in next st* 6 times (54 sts).

Rnds 10-20: sc in each st around.

Fasten off.

EAR FLAP (MAKE 2)

Mark position of Ear Flaps (see page 13). Note: A chain 1 at the beginning of a Row is for turning your work and does not count as a stitch.

Row 1: With tan yarn, attach yarn in 1st st with sc, sc in next 6 sts. Place marker for beginning of row and move marker up as each row is completed (7 sts).

Row 2: ch 1, turn, skip next st, sc in next 6 sts (6 sts).

Row 3: ch 1, turn, skip next st, sc in next 5 sts (5 sts).

Row 4: ch 1, turn, skip next st, sc in next 4 sts (4 sts).

Row 5: ch 1, turn, skip next st, sc in next 3 sts (3 sts).

Row 6: ch 1, turn, skip next st, sc in next 2 sts (2 sts).

Row 7: ch 1, turn, skip next st, sc in next st (1 st).

Fasten off. Weave in end.

EDGE TRIM

Rnd 1: Using tan yarn, attach yarn at center back of Hat with sc. Sc in each st around perimeter of Hat making 3 sts at tip of each Ear Flap. Fasten off.

TWISTED CORD TIE (MAKE 2)

Cut three 24" strands of tan yarn and three 24" strands of brown yarn. Follow instructions on page 14.

ANTLER (MAKE 2)

Each Antler is made in 2 parts.

Part A

With brown yarn, make a magic ring, ch 1.

Rnd 1: 5 sc in ring, pull ring closed tight (5 sts).

Rnd 2: 2 sc in each st around (10 sts).

Rnds 3-?: sc in each st around until piece is 3" long.

Sl st in next st. Fasten off with long tail.

Reindeer

Part B

With brown yarn, make a magic ring, ch 1.

Rnd 1: 5 sc in ring, pull ring closed tight (5 sts).

Rnd 2: 2 sc in each st around (10 sts).

Rnds 3-?: sc in each st around until piece is 1" long.

Sl st in next st. Fasten off with long tail.

NOSE

With red yarn, make a magic ring, ch 1.

Rnd 1: 6 sc in ring, pull ring closed tight (6 sts).

Rnd 2: 2 sc in each st around. Place marker for beginning of rnd and move marker up as each rnd is completed (12 sts).

Rnds 3-4: sc in each st around.

Rnd 5: sc2tog, 6 times, stuffing piece midway around (6 sts).

Fasten off with long tail. Pack in more stuffing with eraser end of pencil. Sew opening shut.

BOW

With red yarn, ch 6 loosely.

Row 1: sc in 2nd chain from hook and in each remaining ch across (5 sts).

Rows 2-3: ch 1, turn, sc in each st across (5 sts).

Rnd 4: sc in each st around next 3 sides. Join with sl st to next st. Fasten off.

Weave ends into wrong side. With a scrap of yarn, tie tightly across center of rectangle. Wrap 1 end around center several times to make a pretty pinched middle. Knot ends together leaving long tails.

EAR (MAKE 2)

With tan yarn, make a magic ring, ch 1.

Rnd 1: 6 sc in ring, pull ring closed tight (6 sts).

Rnd 2: *sc in next 2 sts, 2 sc in next st* 2 times. Place marker for beginning of rnd and move marker up as each rnd is completed (8 sts).

Rnd 3: *sc in next 3 sts, 2 sc in next st* 2 times (10 sts).

Rnd 4: *sc in next 4 sts, 2 sc in next st* 2 times (12 sts).

Rnd 5: *sc in next 5 sts, 2 sc in next st* 2 times (14 sts).

Rnd 6: *sc in next 6 sts, 2 sc in next st* 2 times (16 sts).

Rnd 7: sc in each st around.

Rnd 8: *sc in next 6 sts, sc2tog* 2 times (14 sts).

Rnd 9: *sc in next 5 sts, sc2tog* 2 times (12 sts).

Rnd 10: *sc in next 4 sts, sc2tog* 2 times (10 sts).

Rnd 11: *sc in next 3 sts, sc2tog* 2 times (8 sts).

Sl st in next st. Fasten off with long tail.

ASSEMBLY

Stuff the Antler pieces, pushing stuffing in place with handle of wooden spoon. Sew Antler Part B to side of Part A. Sew Antlers to Hat. Fold Ears in half lengthwise and stitch at open end to hold the crease. Sew Ears, Nose and Bow to Hat. Stack black buttons on white buttons and sew in place for eyes. Weave in ends. ♦

Poinsettia

SUPPLIES

Worsted weight yarn in red (approx. 60 yards) plus small amount of green

Size H/8 (5 mm) crochet hook or size needed to obtain gauge

1 yellow button, 1/2" diameter

Sewing needle & thread

Stitch marker

Yarn needle

GAUGE

7 rnds of sc = 3" diameter circle

HAT

With red yarn, make a magic ring, ch 1.

Rnd 1: 6 sc in ring, pull ring closed tight (6 sts).

Rnd 2: 2 sc in each st around. Place marker for beginning of rnd and move marker up as each rnd is completed (12 sts).

Rnd 3: *sc in next st, 2 sc in next st* 6 times (18 sts).

Rnd 4: *sc in next 2 sts, 2 sc in next st* 6 times (24 sts).

Rnd 5: *sc in next 3 sts, 2 sc in next st* 6 times (30 sts).

Rnd 6: *sc in next 4 sts, 2 sc in next st* 6 times (36 sts).

Rnd 7: *sc in next 5 sts, 2 sc in next st* 6 times (42 sts).

Rnd 8: *sc in next 6 sts, 2 sc in next st* 6 times (48 sts).

Rnd 9: *sc in next 7 sts, 2 sc in next st* 6 times (54 sts).

Rnds 10-20: sc in each st around.

Fasten off.

EAR FLAP (MAKE 2)

Mark position of Ear Flaps (see page 13). Note: A chain 1 at the beginning of a Row is for turning your work and does not count as a stitch.

Row 1: With red yarn, attach yarn in 1st st with sc, sc in next 6 sts. Place marker for beginning of row and move marker up as each row is completed (7 sts).

Row 2: ch 1, turn, skip next st, sc in next 6 sts (6 sts).

Row 3: ch 1, turn, skip next st, sc in next 5 sts (5 sts).

Row 4: ch 1, turn, skip next st, sc in next 4 sts (4 sts).

Row 5: ch 1, turn, skip next st, sc in next 3 sts (3 sts).

Row 6: ch 1, turn, skip next st, sc in next 2 sts (2 sts).

Row 7: ch 1, turn, skip next st, sc in next st (1 st).

Fasten off. Weave in end.

EDGE TRIM

Rnd 1: Using red yarn, attach yarn at center back of Hat with sc. Sc in each st around perimeter of Hat making 3 sts at tip of each Ear Flap. Fasten off.

TWISTED CORD TIE (MAKE 2)

Cut six 24" strands of green yarn. Follow instructions on page 14.

PETAL (MAKE 5)

The Petal is worked around a foundation chain.

With red yarn, ch 8 loosely.

Rnd 1: sc in 2nd ch from hook, hdc in next ch, dc in next 3 ch, hdc in next ch, 3 sc in end ch, hdc in next ch, dc in next 3 ch, hdc in next ch, sc in next ch, sl st in 1st ch. Place marker at beginning of rnd. (16 sts).

Fasten off. Weave in ends.

The tip of each petal will be pointed and the base will be rounded. String all petals together by running a length of yarn on a yarn needle through the base of each petal. Run yarn through first petal again to form a circle, pull tight and knot to hold in shape.

LEAF (MAKE 5)

The Leaf is worked around a foundation chain.

With green yarn, ch 8 loosely.

Rnd 1: sc in 2nd ch from hook, hdc in next ch, dc in next 3 ch, hdc in next ch, 3 sc in end ch, hdc in next ch, dc in next 3 ch, hdc in next ch, sc in next ch, sl st in 1st ch. Place marker at beginning of rnd. (16 sts).

Fasten off. Weave in ends.

The tip of each leaf will be pointed and the base will be rounded. String all leaves together by running a length of yarn on a yarn needle through the base of each leaf. Run yarn through first leaf again to form a circle, pull tight and knot to hold in shape.

ASSEMBLY

Stack Petals on Leaves and sew to Hat. Sew button to center of Petals. Weave in ends. ♦

Christmas Tree

SUPPLIES

Worsted weight yarn in green (approx. 60 yards) and brown (approx. 15 yards) plus small amount of gold and various bright colors (for ornaments)

Size H/8 (5 mm) crochet hook or size needed to obtain gauge

Stitch marker

Yarn needle

GAUGE

7 rnds of sc = 3" diameter circle*
*Crochet in both loops for gauge swatch.

HAT

The hat is worked in **back loops only** (see page 13). This will create a ridged pattern on the tree and ribbing on the brim.

With green yarn, make a magic ring, ch 1.

Rnd 1: 6 sc in ring, pull ring closed tight (6 sts).

Rnd 2: 2 sc in each st around. Place marker for beginning of rnd and move marker up as each rnd is completed (12 sts).

Rnds 3-4: sc in each st around.

Rnd 5: *sc in next st, 2 sc in next st* 6 times (18 sts).

Rnds 6-7: sc in each st around.

Rnd 8: *sc in next 2 sts, 2 sc in next st* 6 times (24 sts).

Rnds 9-11: sc in each st around.

Rnd 12: *sc in next 3 sts, 2 sc in next st* 6 times (30 sts).

Rnds 13-15: sc in each st around.

Rnd 16: *sc in next 4 sts, 2 sc in next st* 6 times (36 sts).

Rnds 17-19: sc in each st around.

Rnd 20: *sc in next 5 sts, 2 sc in next st* 6 times (42 sts).

Rnds 21-24: sc in each st around.

Rnd 25: *sc in next 6 sts, 2 sc in next st* 6 times (48 sts).

Rnds 26-29: sc in each st around.

Rnd 30: *sc in next 7 sts, 2 sc in next st* 6 times (54 sts).

Rnds 31-34: sc in each st around. Fasten off. *Note: Rnd 34 will be the **foundation round** into which the Ribbed Brim is crocheted.*

Ribbed Brim

It can be helpful to go down a hook size for the brim to ensure a snug fit. Otherwise, keep your stitches tight.

You will be working around the hat in short rows that attach to the foundation round (see Figure A). **Remember to work in back loops only!**

Using brown yarn, fasten on at center back of hat with sc.

Row 1: ch 6, sc in 2nd ch from hook and in each remaining ch across (5 sts), sc2tog in next 2 sts of foundation rnd. *Note: The sc2tog is a locking st that attaches the brim rows to the foundation rnd.*

Row 2: turn, skip locking st, sc in each st across (5 sts).

Row 3: ch 1, turn, sc in 2nd st from hook and in each remaining st across (5 sts), sc2tog in next 2 sts of foundation rnd.

Rows 4-54: repeat rows 2-3 around. Fasten off with long tail. Sew 1st and last rows together with whip stitch.

Work in Back Loops Only

5½"

FIGURE A

68 Christmas Tree

STAR (MAKE 2)

With gold yarn, make a magic ring, ch 1.

Rnd 1: 10 sc in ring, pull ring closed tight (10 sts).

Rnd 2: *sl st in next st, ch 4, sl st in 2nd ch from hook, sc in next ch, dc in next ch, sl st in next st* 5 times (5 points).

Fasten off with long tail.

ASSEMBLY

Sew Stars back-to-back at top of Hat, sandwiching tip of Hat between Stars. For ornaments, use double strands of brightly-colored yarn to make French Knots randomly on Hat. (I like to mark their placement beforehand with 1/4" round stickers.) Weave in ends. ♦

Gingerbread Girl

SUPPLIES

Worsted weight yarn in brown (approx. 50 yards) plus small amount of white, red and green

Size H/8 (5 mm) crochet hook or size needed to obtain gauge

2 black buttons, 5/8" diameter

Sewing needle and thread

Stitch marker

Yarn needle

GAUGE

7 rnds of sc = 3" diameter circle

HAT

With brown yarn, make a magic ring, ch 1.

Rnd 1: 6 sc in ring, pull ring closed tight (6 sts).

Rnd 2: 2 sc in each st around. Place marker for beginning of rnd and move marker up as each rnd is completed (12 sts).

Rnd 3: *sc in next st, 2 sc in next st* 6 times (18 sts).

Rnd 4: *sc in next 2 sts, 2 sc in next st* 6 times (24 sts).

Rnd 5: *sc in next 3 sts, 2 sc in next st* 6 times (30 sts).

Rnd 6: *sc in next 4 sts, 2 sc in next st* 6 times (36 sts).

Rnd 7: *sc in next 5 sts, 2 sc in next st* 6 times (42 sts).

Rnd 8: *sc in next 6 sts, 2 sc in next st* 6 times (48 sts).

Rnd 9: *sc in next 7 sts, 2 sc in next st* 6 times (54 sts).

Rnds 10-20: sc in each st around.

Fasten off.

EAR FLAP (MAKE 2)

Mark position of Ear Flaps (see page 13). Note: A chain 1 at the beginning of a Row is for turning your work and does not count as a stitch.

Row 1: With brown yarn, attach yarn in 1st st with sc, sc in next 6 sts. Place marker for beginning of row and move marker up as each row is completed (7 sts).

Row 2: ch 1, turn, skip next st, sc in next 6 sts (6 sts).

Row 3: ch 1, turn, skip next st, sc in next 5 sts (5 sts).

Row 4: ch 1, turn, skip next st, sc in next 4 sts (4 sts).

Row 5: ch 1, turn, skip next st, sc in next 3 sts (3 sts).

Row 6: ch 1, turn, skip next st, sc in next 2 sts (2 sts).

Row 7: ch 1, turn, skip next st, sc in next st (1 st).

Fasten off. Weave in end.

EDGE TRIM

Using white yarn, attach yarn at center back of Hat with sc.

Rnd 1: *3 sc in next st, skip next st, sl st in next st* around.

Fasten off.

TWISTED CORD TIE (MAKE 2)

Cut three 24" strands of red yarn and three 24" strands of green yarn. Follow instructions on page 14.

BOW

With green yarn, ch 8 loosely.

Row 1: sc in 2nd chain from hook and in each remaining ch across (7 sts).

Rows 2-5: ch 1, turn, sc in each st across (7 sts).

Rnd 6: sc in each st around next 3 sides. Join with sl st to next st. Fasten off.

Weave ends into wrong side. With a scrap of yarn, tie tightly across center of rectangle. Wrap 1 end around center several times to make a pretty pinched middle. Knot ends together leaving long tails.

Gingerbread Girl

CHEEKS

With red yarn, make a magic ring, ch 1.

Rnd 1: 6 sc in ring, pull ring closed tight (6 sts).

Rnd 2: 2 sc in each st around. Place marker for beginning of rnd and move marker up as each rnd is completed (12 sts).

Fasten off.

MOUTH

With white yarn, ch 10 loosely. Fasten off with long tail.

UPPER FROSTING

With white yarn, ch 70 loosely. Fasten off with long tail.

ASSEMBLY

Sew mouth in a smiley curve to Hat. Sew Cheeks to Hat. Sew buttons in place for eyes. Sew Upper Frosting in a squiggly line around top of Hat. (Upper Frosting and Mouth can be made with chain stitch embroidery if preferred.) Place Bow in position and pull long tails through to wrong side. Tie Bow to Hat. Weave in ends. ♦

Buckle 'n Belt

The **Buckle 'n Belt** hat can be adapted for several holidays. Instructions are provided below for the **Christmas** version. See photos on page 74 for the colors to use for **St. Patrick's Day** and **Thanksgiving** versions.

SUPPLIES

Worsted weight yarn in red (approx. 55 yards) plus small amount of black, white and gold

Size H/8 (5 mm) crochet hook or size needed to obtain gauge

Lightweight cardboard

Stitch marker

Yarn needle

GAUGE

7 rnds of sc = 3" diameter circle

HAT

With red yarn, make a magic ring, ch 1.

Rnd 1: 6 sc in ring, pull ring closed tight (6 sts).

Rnd 2: 2 sc in each st around. Place marker for beginning of rnd and move marker up as each rnd is completed (12 sts).

Rnd 3: *sc in next st, 2 sc in next st* 6 times (18 sts).

Rnd 4: *sc in next 2 sts, 2 sc in next st* 6 times (24 sts).

Rnd 5: *sc in next 3 sts, 2 sc in next st* 6 times (30 sts).

Rnd 6: *sc in next 4 sts, 2 sc in next st* 6 times (36 sts).

Rnd 7: *sc in next 5 sts, 2 sc in next st* 6 times (42 sts).

Rnd 8: *sc in next 6 sts, 2 sc in next st* 6 times (48 sts).

Rnd 9: *sc in next 7 sts, 2 sc in next st* 6 times (54 sts).

Rnds 10-12: sc in each st around; change to black yarn in last st.

Rnds 13-16: sc in each st around; change to red yarn in last st.

Rnds 17-20: sc in each st around. Fasten off.

EAR FLAP (MAKE 2)

Mark position of Ear Flaps (see page 13). Note: A chain 1 at the beginning of a Row is for turning your work and does not count as a stitch.

Row 1: With red yarn, attach yarn in 1st st with sc, sc in next 6 sts. Place marker for beginning of row and move marker up as each row is completed (7 sts).

Row 2: ch 1, turn, skip next st, sc in next 6 sts (6 sts).

Row 3: ch 1, turn, skip next st, sc in next 5 sts (5 sts).

Row 4: ch 1, turn, skip next st, sc in next 4 sts (4 sts).

Row 5: ch 1, turn, skip next st, sc in next 3 sts (3 sts).

Row 6: ch 1, turn, skip next st, sc in next 2 sts (2 sts).

Row 7: ch 1, turn, skip next st, sc in next st (1 st).

Fasten off. Weave in end.

EDGE TRIM

Rnd 1: Using white yarn, attach yarn at center back of Hat with sc. Sc in each st around perimeter of Hat making 3 sts at tip of each Ear Flap. Fasten off.

TWISTED CORD TIE (MAKE 2)

Cut three 24" strands of red yarn and three 24" strands of white yarn. Follow instructions on page 14.

SMALL POM POM (MAKE 2)

With white yarn, follow instructions on page 15.

74 Buckle 'n Belt

LARGE POM POM

With white yarn, follow instructions on page 15.

ASSEMBLY

Using gold yarn, embroider buckle with chain stitch embroidery (see page 17). Place Large Pom Pom in position and pull long tails through to wrong side. Tie Pom Pom to Hat. Weave in ends. ♦

Leprechaun

Santa

Pilgrim

Party Hat

The Party Hat is fun for New Year's Eve or birthdays. Two topper options are provided: a Pom Pom or Curlicues. Take your pick!

SUPPLIES

Worsted weight yarn in purple (approx. 20 yards) plus small amount of orange, green, pink and turquoise

Size H/8 (5 mm) crochet hook or size needed to obtain gauge

9" x 12" sheet of purple craft foam

Craft glue

Stapler

Stitch marker

Yarn needle

GAUGE

7 rnds of sc = 3" diameter circle

HAT

With purple yarn, make a magic ring, ch 1.

Rnd 1: 4 sc in ring, pull ring closed almost tight (4 sts). *Note: Don't pull ring too tight if the Curlicue topper is used. You will need room to pull 8 yarn tails through the ring.*

Rnd 2: *sc in next st, 2 sc in next st* 2 times. Place marker for beginning of rnd and move marker up as each rnd is completed (6 sts).

Rnd 3: *sc in next 2 sts, 2 sc in next st* 2 times (8 sts).

Rnd 4: *sc in next 3 sts, 2 sc in next st* 2 times (10 sts).

Rnd 5: *sc in next 4 sts, 2 sc in next st* 2 times (12 sts).

Rnd 6: *sc in next 5 sts, 2 sc in next st* 2 times (14 sts).

Rnd 7: *sc in next 6 sts, 2 sc in next st* 2 times (16 sts).

Rnd 8: *sc in next 7 sts, 2 sc in next st* 2 times (18 sts).

Rnd 9: *sc in next 8 sts, 2 sc in next st* 2 times (20 sts).

Rnd 10: *sc in next 9 sts, 2 sc in next st* 2 times (22 sts).

Rnd 11: *sc in next 10 sts, 2 sc in next st* 2 times (24 sts).

Rnd 12: *sc in next 11 sts, 2 sc in next st* 2 times (26 sts).

Rnd 13: *sc in next 12 sts, 2 sc in next st* 2 times (28 sts).

Rnd 14: *sc in next 13 sts, 2 sc in next st* 2 times (30 sts).

Rnd 15: *sc in next 14 sts, 2 sc in next st* 2 times (32 sts).

Rnd 16: *sc in next 15 sts, 2 sc in next st* 2 times (34 sts).

Rnd 17: *sc in next 16 sts, 2 sc in next st* 2 times (36 sts).

Rnd 18: *sc in next 18 sts, 2 sc in next st* 2 times (38 sts).

Sl st in next st. Fasten off with long tail.

EDGE TRIM

Using orange yarn, attach yarn at center back of Hat with sc.

Rnd 1: *5 sc in next st, skip next st, sl st in next st* around.

Fasten off.

TWISTED CORD TIE (MAKE 2)

Cut two 36" strands of pink yarn and two 36" strands of turquoise yarn. Follow twisting instructions on page 14 but note the following changes: There will be 4 strands of yarn for each tie. Pull them through underside of Edge Trim and divide into 2 groups of 4 strands. Tie knots 12" from edge of Hat.

POLKA DOT (MAKE 6)

Make 2 from each of the following colors: pink, turquoise and green.

Make a magic ring, ch 1.

Rnd 1: 5 sc in ring, pull ring closed tight (5 sts).

Sl st in next st. Fasten off with long tail.

Party Hat

CURLICUE (MAKE 4)

Make 1 from each of the following colors: orange, pink, turquoise and green.

Ch 20 loosely.

Row 1: sc in 2nd ch from hook and in each ch across (19 sts).

Fasten off. Curl with fingers into a tight spiral.

SMALL POM POM

With orange yarn, use Small Pom Pom template but follow instructions for Medium and Large Pom Poms (see page 15).

LINING

Using Template on page 81, cut 1 lining piece from craft foam.

ASSEMBLY

If Pom Pom topper is used, place Pom Pom on top of Hat and pull long tails through to wrong side. Tie Pom Pom to Hat.

If Curlicue topper is used, pull Curlicue tails through stitch at top of Hat. Turn Hat inside out, tie tails together and trim ends close to knot. Turn Hat right side out.

Coil lining into a cone, insert into Hat and adjust for a good fit. Remove from Hat and staple to hold cone shape. Apply glue to outside of cone and insert in Hat. Let dry.

Weave in ends. ♦

Pom Pom Topper

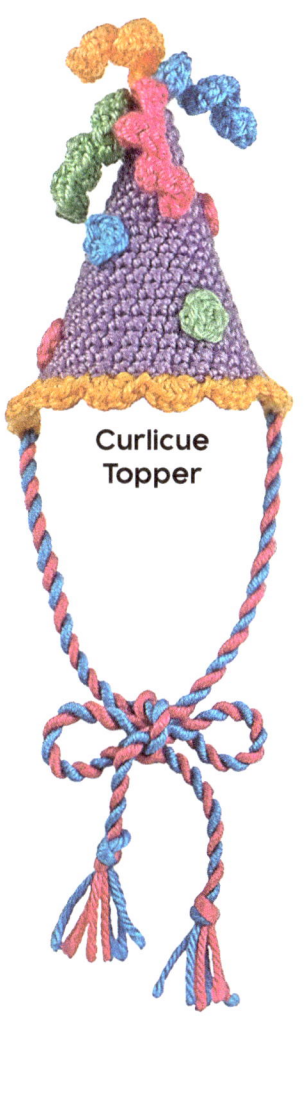

Curlicue Topper

Resources

YARN

Caron Yarn
caron.com
 Simply Soft

Lion Brand
lionbrand.com
 Vanna's Choice

Red Heart
redheart.com
 Soft

Michaels
michaels.com
 Caron *Simply Soft*
 Lion Brand *Vanna's Choice*
 Red Heart *Soft*

Joann Fabric and Craft Stores
joann.com
 Caron *Simply Soft*
 Lion Brand *Vanna's Choice*
 Red Heart *Soft*

NOTIONS

Joann Fabric and Craft Stores
joann.com
 Clover *Soft Touch Crochet Hook*
 Disappearing ink marking pen
 Jumbo tapestry needles
 Locking stitch markers
 Knitting counter
 White star sequins

BUTTONS

Create for Less
createforless.com

Lots of Buttons
lotsofbuttons.com

VIDEO TUTORIALS

YouTube!
youtube.com
 Search on the name of the stitch or technique you want to learn.

Pinterest
pinterest.com/LindalooEnt/
 Visit my Pinterest page to view video tutorials for the stitches and techniques used in this book. Look for the boards named "Amigurumi Tutorials" and "Embroidery Tutorials".

Templates

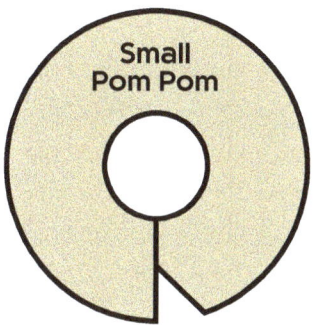
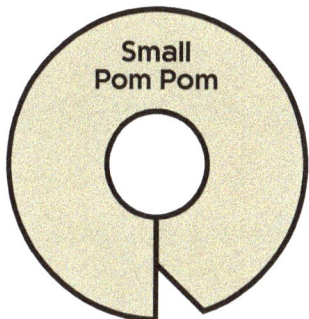
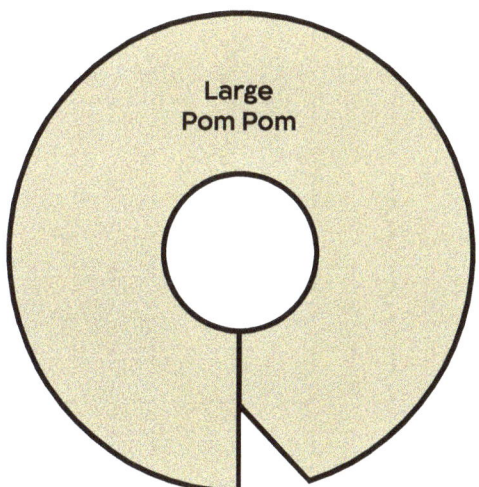
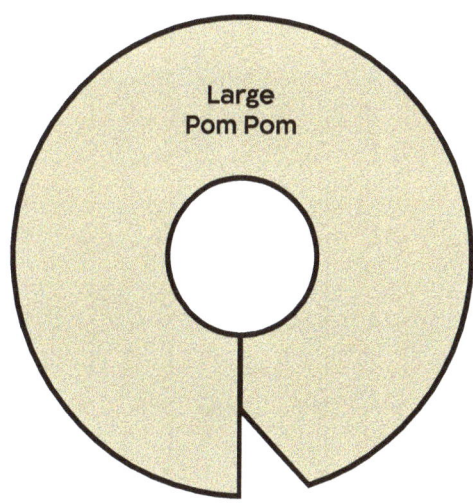

Templates 81

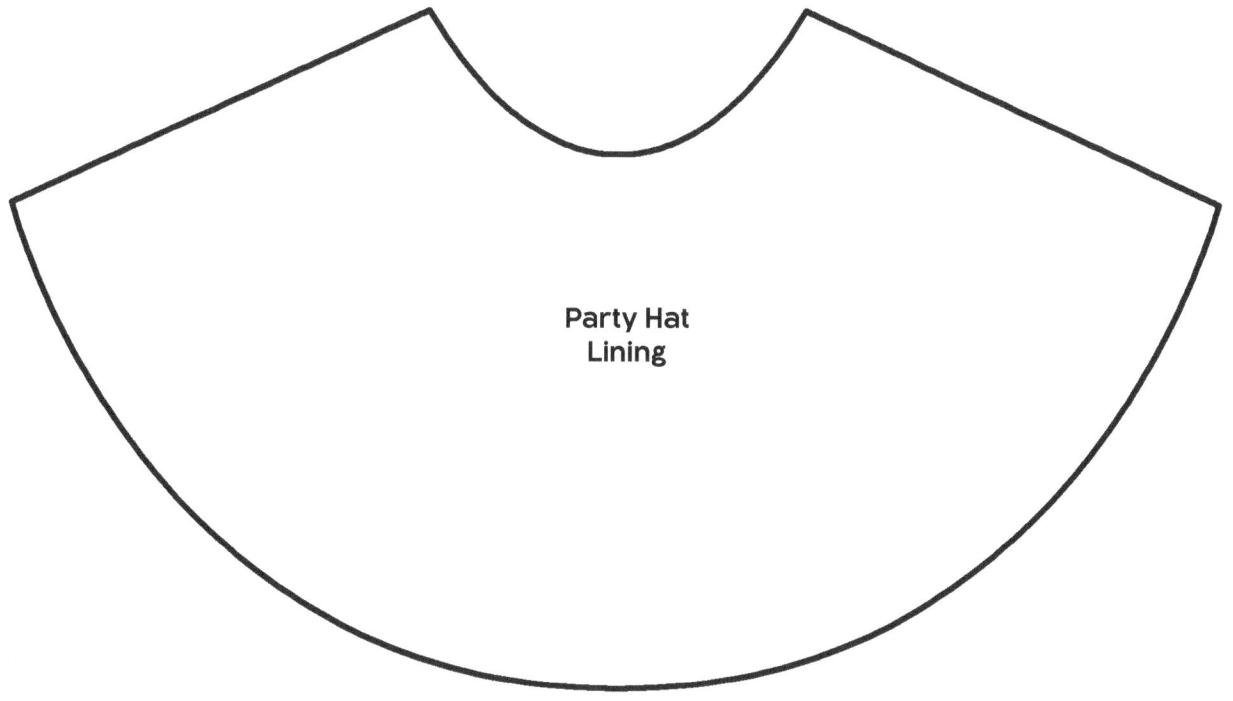

Party Hat Lining

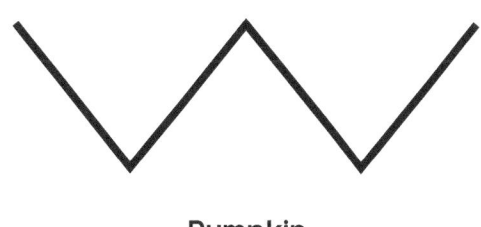

Pumpkin Mouth

Featured Yarn

The following yarns were used for these holiday hats.

Valentine

Red Heart "Soft Baby Steps"

    Color: Strawberry, #9702

Red Heart "Soft"

    Color: Really Red, #9925

    Color: White, #4600

Hearts Around

Red Heart "Soft Baby Steps"

    Color: Strawberry, #9702

Red Heart "Soft"

    Color: Wine, #4608

Shamrock

Caron "Simply Soft"

    Color: Pistachio, #0003

Red Heart "Soft"

    Color: Dark Leaf, #9523

Top Hat

• *St. Patrick's Day*

Lion Brand "Vanna's Choice"

    Color: Fern, #171

    Color: Black, #153

    Color: Mustard, #158

• *Independence Day*

Red Heart "Soft"

    Color: Really Red, #9925

    Color: Navy, #4604

• *Thanksgiving*

Red Heart "Soft"

    Color: Toast, #1882

    Color: Tangerine, #4422

    Color: Lt. Grey Heather, #9440

• *New Year's Eve*

Red Heart "Soft Baby Steps"

    Color: Strawberry, #9702

Funky Bunny

Caron "Simply Soft"

    Color: Lavender Blue, #9756

    Color: Lemonade, #9776

    Color: Strawberry, #0015

    Color: Limelight, #9607

Easter Bonnet

Caron "Simply Soft"

    Color: White, #9701

    Color: Lavender Blue, #9756

    Color: Strawberry, #0015

    Color: Sage, #9705

    Color: Sunshine, #9755

Easter Chick

Red Heart "Soft"

    Color: Seafoam, #9520

Caron "Simply Soft"

    Color: Gold, #9782

Stars & Stripes

Red Heart "Soft"

    Color: Really Red, #9925

    Color: White, #4600

    Color: Navy, #4604

Pumpkin

Red Heart "Soft"

    Color: Tangerine, #4422

    Color: Toast, #1882

    Color: Guacamole, #4420

    Color: Black, #4614

Featured Yarn

Witch

Lion Brand "Vanna's Choice"
- Color: Eggplant, #145
- Color: Fern, #171

Black Cat

Caron "Simply Soft"
- Color: Black, #9727
- Color: Mango, #9605
- Color: White, #9701

Devil

Red Heart "Soft"
- Color: Really Red, #9925
- Color: Black, #4614

Turkey

Red Heart "Soft"
- Color: Toast, #1882
- Color: Really Red, #9925
- Color: Tangerine, #4422

Caron "Simply Soft"
- Color: Sunshine, #9755

Santa

Caron "Simply Soft"
- Color: Harvest Red, #9763
- Color: White, #9701

Reindeer

Red Heart "Soft"
- Color: Wheat, #9388
- Color: Toast, #1882
- Color: Really Red, #9925

Poinsettia

Red Heart "Soft"
- Color: Really Red, #9925
- Color: Dark Leaf, #9523

Christmas Tree

Lion Brand "Vanna's Choice"
- Color: Kelly Green, #172
- Color: Chocolate, #126
- Color: Mustard, #158

Gingerbread Girl

Red Heart "Soft"
- Color: Toast, #1882
- Color: White, #4600
- Color: Really Red, #9925
- Color: Guacamole, #4420

Buckle 'n Belt

- *Christmas*

Red Heart "Soft"
- Color: Really Red, #9925

- Color: White, #4600
- Color: Black, #4614

Lion Brand "Vanna's Choice"
- Color: Mustard, #158

- *St. Patrick's Day*

Lion Brand "Vanna's Choice"
- Color: Fern, #171
- Color: Black, #153
- Color: Mustard, #158

- *Thanksgiving*

Red Heart "Soft"
- Color: Toast, #1882
- Color: Tangerine, #4422
- Color: Lt. Grey Heather, #9440

Party Hat

Red Heart "Soft"
- Color: Lilac, #9528

Caron "Simply Soft"
- Color: Watermelon, #9604
- Color: Blue Mint, #9608
- Color: Limelight, #9607
- Color: Mango, #9605

Other books by Linda Wright

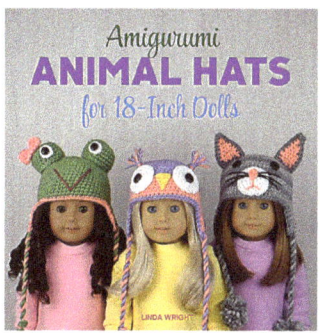

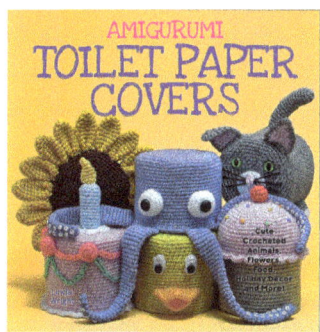

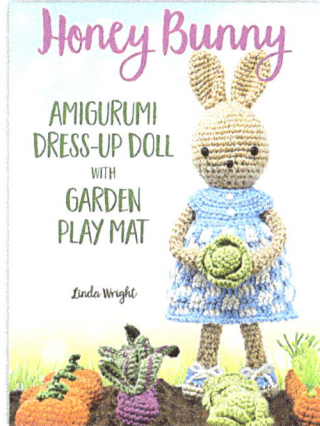

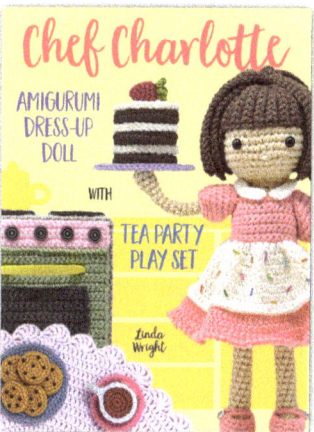

LINDA WRIGHT studied textiles and clothing design at the Pennsylvania State University. She is the author of various handicraft books including the groundbreaking *Toilet Paper Origami*, its companion book, *Toilet Paper Origami On a Roll* and numerous works of amigurumi-style crochet.

Notes

www.ingramcontent.com/pod-product-compliance
Lightning Source LLC
Chambersburg PA
CBHW040041180426
PP18159100001B/1